A SHORT ACCOUNT

OF THE

HEBREW TENSES

A SHORT ACCOUNT

OF THE

HEBREW TENSES

BY

THE REV. R. H. KENNETT, M.A.

FELLOW AND LECTURER OF QUEENS' COLLEGE, CAMBRIDGE
UNIVERSITY LECTURER IN ARAMAIC

CAMBRIDGE:
AT THE UNIVERSITY PRESS
1901

[All Rights reserved.]

CAMBRIDGE
UNIVERSITY PRESS

University Printing House, Cambridge CB2 8BS, United Kingdom

Published in the United States of America by Cambridge University Press, New York

Cambridge University Press is part of the University of Cambridge.

It furthers the University's mission by disseminating knowledge in the pursuit of
education, learning and research at the highest international levels of excellence.

www.cambridge.org
Information on this title: www.cambridge.org/9781107645417

First published 1901
First paperback edition 2014

A catalogue record for this publication is available from the British Library

ISBN 978-1-107-64541-7 Paperback

PREFACE.

THE present volume is an attempt to give an account of the nature and use of the Tenses in Hebrew in a form suitable for those who have but recently begun the study of the language, and who have not attained to such proficiency as will enable them to use with advantage Professor Driver's indispensable book. I have commonly found in teaching, that a student's chief difficulty in the Hebrew verbs is to grasp the meaning which they conveyed to the minds of the Hebrews themselves; that is to say, there is a tendency to assign as equivalents to each of the Hebrew Tenses a certain number of Latin or English forms by which that particular Tense may commonly be translated. The result is a failure to perceive many of those fine shades of meaning, which give such life and vigour to the language of the Old Testament.

The difficulty in the use of the Hebrew verbs lies solely in the point of view, so absolutely different from our own, from which the Hebrews regarded an action; the *time*, which with us is the first consideration, as the very word 'tense' shews, being to them a matter of secondary importance. It is, therefore, essential that a student should clearly grasp, not so much the Latin or English forms which may be used in translating each of the Hebrew Tenses, but rather the aspect of each action, as it presented itself to a Hebrew's mind.

To deal adequately, however, with such a subject is beyond the limits of a grammar intended for the use of students, and yet no real progress can be made in Hebrew until it is mastered.

In treating of a subject so wide, in which the natural divisions are few, and often slightly marked, it is not easy to make a selection, and one is sorely tempted to multiply examples at the expense of brevity. I trust that the illustrations which are printed under the several headings will be sufficient for learners, but, lest I may be thought too dogmatic in my statements or in my omissions, I have dealt with some of the vexed questions in additional notes.

My heartiest thanks are due to my friend Mr F. C. Burkitt for kindly reading through the greater part of my notes in manuscript, and for many valuable suggestions. It is, however, only fair to him to say that he is in no wise responsible for any of the opinions here set forth.

ROBERT H. KENNETT.

QUEENS' COLLEGE,
    January 16, 1901.

A SHORT ACCOUNT OF THE HEBREW TENSES.

THE name 'tenses' as applied to Hebrew verbs is misleading. The so-called Hebrew 'tenses' do not express the *time* but merely the *state* of an action. Indeed were it not for the confusion that would arise through the application of the term 'state' to both nouns and verbs, 'states' would be a far better designation than 'tenses.' It must always be borne in mind that it is impossible to translate a Hebrew verb into English without employing a limitation (viz. of time) which is entirely absent in the Hebrew. The ancient Hebrews never thought of an action as past, present, or future, but simply as *perfect*, i.e. complete, or *imperfect*, i.e. as in course of development. When we say that a certain Hebrew tense corresponds to a Perfect, Pluperfect, or Future in English, we do not mean that the Hebrews thought of it as Perfect, Pluperfect, or Future, but merely that it must be so translated in English. The *time* of an action the Hebrews did not attempt to express by any verbal form.

K.   1

THE PERFECT.

The fundamental idea denoted by the Perfect is that of a completed act; and this idea underlies all its various uses. Thus the Perfect is used to describe the following classes of actions:

I. Actions completed at a definite moment in the past: e.g.

בָּרָא אֱלֹהִים אֵת הַשָּׁמַיִם וְאֵת הָאָרֶץ

God created the heavens and the earth (Gen. i. 1)

מַיִם שָׁאַל חָלָב נָתְנָה

Water he asked, milk she gave (Judges v. 25)

II. Actions completed in the past of which the effect remains: e.g.

הוֹשִׁיעָה לוֹ יְמִינוֹ וּזְרוֹעַ קָדְשׁוֹ

His right hand and His holy arm have gained Him the victory (Ps. xcviii. 1)

הֵמַר שַׁדַּי לִי מְאֹד

Shaddai has brought sore trouble upon me (Ruth i. 20)

III. Actions completed in the immediate past, in which case the Perfect passes over into the meaning of the Present: e.g.

כֹּה אָמַר יהוה

Thus saith Jehovah (passim)

הֲרִמֹתִי יָדִי אֶל־יהוה אֵל עֶלְיוֹן

I lift up my hand to Jehovah God most high (Gen. xiv. 22)

and similarly,

יָדַעְתִּי *I know,* זָכַרְתִּי *I remember.*

N.B. The Perfect of so-called 'stative' verbs is naturally used to express a state complete in the present: e.g.

קָטֹנְתִּי *I am small,* אָהַבְתִּי *I love,* שָׂנֵאתִי *I hate.*

לֹא קָצְרָה יַד יהוה מֵהוֹשִׁיעַ וְלֹא כָבְדָה אָזְנוֹ מִשְּׁמוֹעַ

Jehovah's hand is not too short to save, nor His ear too dull to hear (Isaiah lix. 1)

IV. Actions completed in the future, which in Latin would be expressed by the Future Perfect or Subjunctive Perfect: e.g.

וְאִם־כֹּה אֹמַר לָעֶלֶם......לֵךְ כִּי שִׁלַּחֲךָ יהוה

But if I say thus to the youth......, go, for Jehovah will have sent thee away (1 Sam. xx. 22)

אַל־תַּעֲצָר־לִי לִרְכֹּב כִּי אִם־אָמַרְתִּי לָךְ

I will not have thee stop driving unless I tell thee (shall have told thee) (2 Kings iv. 24)

יְבַקְשׁוּ אֶת־אֲדֹנֶיךָ פֶּן־נְשָׂאוֹ רוּחַ יהוה

Let them seek thy master, lest the wind of Jehovah may have taken him up (2 Kings ii. 16)

1—2

V.   Actions completed before some definite point of
time in the past, which in Latin would be expressed by
the Pluperfect: e.g.

וַיִּשְׁבֹּת בַּיּוֹם הַשְּׁבִיעִי מִכָּל־מְלַאכְתּוֹ אֲשֶׁר עָשָׂה

*And He desisted on the seventh day from all His work
which He had done* (Gen. ii. 2)

וְרָחֵל לָקְחָה אֶת־הַתְּרָפִים

Now Rachel had taken the teraphim (Gen. xxxi. 34)

לְשֵׁמַע אֹזֶן שְׁמַעְתִּיךָ וְעַתָּה עֵינִי רָאָתְךָ

*By the mere hearing of the ear had I heard of Thee, but
now my own eye has seen Thee* (Job xlii. 5)

N.B.   It must not however be forgotten that, although
the Perfect may frequently be translated by our Pluperfect,
yet the Pluperfect idea is foreign to Hebrew thought.   A
Hebrew merely stated the *completion* of an action, and
left the *time* of its completion to be inferred from the
context.   Thus in the first of the three examples given
above the verb עָשָׂה merely states the completion of the
act of doing.   It is obvious from the context that this act
of doing was completed before God desisted from the work
of creation.   So likewise in the second illustration it is
merely stated that Rachel took the teraphim, the context
making it sufficiently clear that she took them before her
father began to look for them.

VI.   Actions of which the time is quite indefinite, the
completion of the single act alone being regarded[1]: e.g.

---

[1] This is the so-called Perfect of Experience: it scarcely occurs in
ordinary prose.

יָבֵשׁ חָצִיר נָבֵל צִיץ כִּי רוּחַ יהוה נָשְׁבָה בּוֹ

Grass withers, flower fades, when Jehovah's wind has blown upon it (Isaiah xl. 7)

חָתַר בַּחֹשֶׁךְ בָּתִּים

He breaks into houses in the dark (Job xxiv. 16)

VII. Actions the sphere of which belongs to the future, the certainty with which they are regarded being thus expressed[1]: e.g.

חֶלְקַת הַשָּׂדֶה......מָכְרָה נָעֳמִי

Naomi is selling (has determined to sell)......the plot of land (Ruth iv. 3)

הַשָּׂדֶה נָתַתִּי לָךְ

The whole field I give thee (Gen. xxiii. 11)

---

[1] This Perfect of Certainty is frequent in the writings of the Prophets, and is therefore sometimes called the Prophetic Perfect. **Examples** of its use are: לְמַעַנְכֶם שִׁלַּחְתִּי בָבֶלָה *For your sake will I send to Babylon* (Isaiah xliii. 14); בִּלַּע הַמָּוֶת לָנֶצַח *He will annihilate death for ever* (Isaiah xxv. 8).

In an interrogative sentence the Perfect of Certainty acquires a meaning resembling that of the Deliberative Subjunctive in Greek: e.g. הֶחֳדַלְתִּי אֶת־דִּשְׁנִי *Am I to leave my fatness?* (Judges ix. 9); and, somewhat similarly, עַד־מָתַי מֵאַנְתָּ *How long refusest thou?* (Ex. x. 3). This latter use of the Perfect, however, is rare, and some of the instances which may be assigned to it are capable of a different explanation: thus in the quotation from Exodus x. 3 the Perfect מֵאַנְתָּ may be explained on the analogy of 'stative' verbs (see above, § III, note) or even as a Future Perfect.

N.B. It must be remembered that, as there is no *time* in the Hebrew tenses, the Perfect may refer to the *future equally well as to the past.* It is incorrect to say that the Hebrew said 'I have done' when he meant 'I will do': in reality he merely described the completion of the act of doing *without specifying the time.* But as there is no more emphatic way of predicting an event still future than by describing its result (see, for example, Isaiah xiii., where the certainty of the fall of Babylon is brought out by the description of its future desolation), so an event which is obviously future, when described as completed, is impressed upon the hearer's mind as certain.

VIII.   Hypothetical actions, completed

(*a*)   at or before some definite time in the past: e.g.

לוּ הַחֲיִתֶם אוֹתָם לֹא הָרַגְתִּי אֶתְכֶם

If ye had saved them alive, I would not have slain you (I would not slay you)[1] (Judges viii. 19)

לוּלֵא הִתְמַהְמָהְנוּ כִּי עַתָּה שַׁבְנוּ זֶה פַּעֲמָיִם

If we had not delayed, we might by this time have returned twice over[2] (Gen. xliii. 10)

---

[1] The use of the Perfect הָרַגְתִּי in the *apodosis* to express an action still future may be explained on the analogy of the Perfect of Certainty.

[2] The use of the Perfect in the *apodosis* of this sentence does not materially differ from its use in the *protasis*. Thus the Perfect שַׁבְנוּ expresses the hypothetical completion of the act of return at some moment in the past in consequence of a previous hypothetical action.

To this heading may be assigned such a sentence as Genesis xxi. 7 מִי מִלֵּל לְאַבְרָהָם הֵינִיקָה בָנִים שָׂרָה *Who would have said to Abraham* (sc. if he had known the circumstances), *Sarah is to suckle children ?*

(*b*)   in the past, but with effect continuing into the present : e.g.

אִם־עָשִׂיתִי זֹאת......יְרֹדֹּף¹ אוֹיֵב נַפְשִׁי

If I have done this (the guilt of which still continues)......
then let an enemy persecute my soul (Ps. vii. 4, 6)

אִם־יהוה הֱסִיתְךָ בִי יָרַח מִנְחָה

If it be Jehovah that has stirred thee up against me,
let him smell an offering (1 Sam. xxvi. 19)

(*c*)   in the future : e.g.

אִם־זָרְחָה הַשֶּׁמֶשׁ עָלָיו דָּמִים לוֹ

If the sun shall have risen upon him, there shall be
bloodguiltiness for him (Ex. xxii. 2)

אִם־רָחַץ אֲדֹנָי אֵת צֹאַת בְּנוֹת צִיּוֹן

If (when) the Lord shall have washed away the filth of
the daughters of Sion (Isaiah iv. 4)

(*d*)   at some indefinite time or times, i.e. when the verb in the *apodosis* expresses what is habitual : e.g.

וְאִם־בָּא לִרְאוֹת שָׁוְא יְדַבֵּר

And if he come (whenever he may have come) to see, he
speaks (is wont to speak) that which is vain

(Ps. xli. 7)

וְאִם־זָכַרְתִּי וְנִבְהָלְתִּי

And whenever I think (sc. of the injustice in the world),
I am panic-stricken (Job xxi. 6)

---

¹ Point thus.

IX. Actions the completion of which is desired[1],

(a) in the past: e.g.

לוּ־מַתְנוּ בְּאֶרֶץ מִצְרַיִם

Would that we had died in the land of Egypt! (i.e. If we had died in the land of Egypt, it had been well with us)

(Numbers xiv. 2)

(b) in the present: e.g.

מִי־יִתֵּן יָדַעְתִּי

O that I knew! (i.e. Who will give—O that one would give—the state described by the word יָדַעְתִּי)

(Job xxiii. 3)

(c) in the future: e.g.

לוּא־קָרַעְתָּ שָׁמַיִם

O that thou wouldest rend the heavens! (Isaiah lxiii. 19)

X. The Perfect is also frequently used in sentences which western idiom puts into a hypothetical form, but which, technically, are scarcely hypothetical in Hebrew. In such sentences the division into *protasis* and *apodosis* is misleading: they are in reality coordinate clauses, and the graphic Hebrew idiom with its absolute method of expression, that disdains saving clauses and particles,

---

[1] This must not be understood as implying a belief in the so-called 'Precative' Perfect, the existence of which in Hebrew is extremely doubtful. The Perfect, though it may express confident expectation, does not of itself express a wish. The illustrations given above under (a) and (c) are in reality merely the *protases* of hypothetical sentences of which the *apodoses* are suppressed.

introduces what is in reality only hypothetical or possible
as though it were fact or certainty[1]. Illustrations are

מָצָא אִשָּׁה מָצָא טוֹב

If one has found a wife, one has found a good thing
(Prov. xviii. 22)

[In this sentence the two clauses are coordinate. The
Hebrew, so to speak, paints a picture of the finding of a
wife as an accomplished fact, and likewise the finding of
a good thing as parallel to it, the *time* being quite indefinite.]

הֲנִסָּה דָבָר אֵלֶיךָ תִּלְאֶה[2]

*If one were to attempt to speak to thee, wouldest thou be
wearied?* (Anglice *would it be too much for thee?*)
(Job iv. 2)

הֲלֹא נִסַּע יִתְרָם (? יְתֵדָם) בָּם יָמוּתוּ[2]

*When their cord (? tent-peg) is plucked up in them,
do they not die?* (Job iv. 21)

---

[1] Similar sentences, viz. hypothetical in English but not in Hebrew,
are found even where there is no verb in the first clause: e.g.
וְלֹא יֻתַּן־נָא לְעַבְדְּךָ מַשָּׂא *Then if not* (i.e. assuming that the refusal to
accept a present is unalterable), *let there be given to thy servant a load*, etc.
(2 Kings v. 17), cf. 2 Kings x. 15 ; and similarly with the Participle : e.g.
הִנֵּה יהוה עֹשֶׂה אֲרֻבּוֹת בַּשָּׁמַיִם הֲיִהְיֶה הַדָּבָר הַזֶּה *Supposing that Jehovah
be even now making windows in the heavens, can such a thing come to pass?*
(2 Kings vii. 2).

[2] In this instance the interrogative particle, although placed at the
head of the sentence, really belongs to the second verb, or perhaps it
would be more true to say that the interrogative particle belongs to the
whole sense conveyed by the two closely coordinated clauses.

THE IMPERFECT.

The Imperfect in its fundamental meaning denotes actions as incomplete, i.e. as in process of development. It does not express the mere *continuance* of an action, which would be expressed by the Participle, but the *development* of it *from its beginning* towards its completion. Whereas the Perfect, so to speak, paints a single picture of an action as completed, the Imperfect paints a series of pictures. Thus in the words נָפְלָה בָבֶל we have a picture of the fall of Babylon as an accomplished fact, without any specification of the time ; in תִּפֹּל בָּבֶל, on the other hand, we have, as it were, a cinematographic representation of the fall of Babylon, stopping short however of the complete end. In the Imperfect, as in the Perfect, there is no definition of *time*: the *time* of an action denoted by it can only be inferred from the context.

I.   The Imperfect is accordingly used to denote actions regarded as in process of development,

(*a*)   in the past: e.g.

וְהַבַּיִת יִמָּלֵא עָשָׁן

And the house began to fill (and kept filling) *with smoke*
(Isaiah vi. 4)

וּבְכָל־אֶרֶץ מִצְרַיִם תִּשָּׁחֵת הָאָרֶץ

And in all the land of Egypt the land began to be destroyed
(implying that the destruction went on from one stage
to another) (Exodus viii. 20)[1]

---

[1] Similarly the Imperfect is commonly used after אָז 'then' and טֶרֶם 'not yet,' since both words call attention to the origin and

(*b*) in the present : e.g.

יִנָּטוּ צִלְלֵי־עָרֶב

The evening shadows are beginning to lengthen
(Jerem. vi. 4)

שָׁמְעוּ עַמִּים יִרְגָּזוּן

The peoples have heard, they begin to tremble (Exodus xv. 14)[1]

(*c*) in the future : e.g.

יהוה בְּמִשְׁפָּט יָבוֹא

Jehovah will enter into judgment (Isaiah iii. 14)

אָז תִּפָּקַחְנָה עֵינֵי עִוְרִים

Then shall the eyes of the blind be opened (Isaiah xxxv. 5)

N.B. Since in the case of actions still future their *development* rather than their *completion* is usually contemplated, the Imperfect is naturally used to denote such actions; but if the *completion* of a future act is contemplated, the Perfect is used. It must be clearly understood that the Imperfect conveys *no idea of time,*

---

development of the action following : e.g. אָז יָשִׁיר מֹשֶׁה *Then Moses began to sing* (Exodus xv. 1) ; בְּטֶרֶם תָּחִיל יָלָדָה *Before she travailed* (she had not yet begun to travail) *she brought forth* (Isaiah lxvi. 7).

[1] Here belongs such an expression as אֶרְאֶנּוּ וְלֹא עַתָּה *I see him but not now* (Num. xxiv. 17). In this case אֶרְאֶנּוּ is not a simple Present, *which is never expressed by the Imperfect* but by the Participle. The Imperfect here conveys the idea, in a graphic manner, of the vision flashing upon the seer and becoming more and more vivid. This explanation seems preferable to that which would make אֶרְאֶנּוּ a simple Future.

and is used in expressing future actions only because such
actions for the most part present themselves to our minds
as in process of development rather than as complete.
That this is the case is clear from the fact that, when
it is necessary to emphasize the *completion* of a future
action, the Perfect is used.

II. Since there is no idea of time in the Hebrew
tenses, which have regard merely to the *state* of an action,
whether from a past, present, or future standpoint, the
Imperfect, which, as we have seen, is used to denote
actions still future from some standpoint in the present,
is naturally used to denote those actions also which may
be regarded as future from some standpoint in the past.
Accordingly the Future Participle of the Latin with the
past tense of the verb 'to be' is expressed in Hebrew by
the Imperfect : e.g.

$$\text{וֶאֱלִישָׁע חָלָה אֶת־חָלְיוֹ אֲשֶׁר יָמוּת בּוֹ}$$

*Now Elisha was fallen sick of his sickness whereof
he was to die* (2 Kings xiii. 14)

$$\text{וַיִּקַּח אֶת־בְּנוֹ הַבְּכוֹר אֲשֶׁר־יִמְלֹךְ תַּחְתָּיו}$$

And he took his eldest son who was to reign (Anglice
would have reigned) *after him* (2 Kings iii. 27)

$$\text{הֲיָדוֹעַ נֵדַע כִּי יֹאמַר}$$

Were we to know that he would say, etc. ? (Gen. xliii. 7)

$$\text{הַכְּמוֹת נָבָל יָמוּת אַבְנֵר}$$

Was Abner to die (i.e. *Who would have said that Abner
would die*) *like a knave ?* (2 Sam. iii. 33)

לְמָּה לֹא מֵרֶחֶם אָמוּת

Why could I not have died (more literally 'Why was I not in the condition of being about to die') *from the womb ?* (Job iii. 11)

N.B. In the above examples, although English idiom requires a variety of renderings, the fundamental meaning of the Imperfect is never set aside. Thus, to refer again to our previous illustration of its meaning in connexion with the first of the four passages quoted above, יָמוּת is, so to speak, a cinematographic representation of Elisha's death, stopping short however of the complete end. Since the narrator has made it clear that at the time of his writing Elisha is dead, and he yet represents the act of dying as in process of development rather than as complete, his readers at once understand that the standpoint from which this representation begins is some point of time before Elisha's death.

III. The fundamental meaning of the Imperfect being development, by a slight extension of its original scope it is used to denote actions which progress from stage to stage, but do not once for all attain to completion, hence repeated or customary acts, whether

(a) in the past : e.g.

וְאֵד יַעֲלֶה מִן־הָאָרֶץ

And a mist used to go up from the earth (Gen. ii. 6)

וּמֹשֶׁה יִקַּח אֶת־הָאֹהֶל

Now Moses used to take the tent (Ex. xxxiii. 7)

(*b*)   or in the present: e.g.

בִּנְאוֹת דֶּשֶׁא יַרְבִּיצֵנִי

In grassy pastures He makes me lie (Ps. xxiii. 2)

חֹרְשֵׁי אָוֶן וְזֹרְעֵי עָמָל יִקְצְרֻהוּ

Those who plough unprofitableness and sow trouble reap it
(i.e. what they have sown) (Job iv. 8)

(*c*)   or in the future: e.g.

מִדֵּי שַׁבָּת בְּשַׁבַּתּוֹ יָבוֹא כָל־בָּשָׂר לְהִשְׁתַּחֲוֹת

Sabbath by sabbath shall all flesh come to worship
(Isaiah lxvi. 23)

מַעֲשֵׂי יְדֵיהֶם יְבַלּוּ בְחִירָי

The work of their hands my chosen ones shall (habitually)
enjoy to the full (Isaiah lxv. 22)

IV.   Closely connected with those uses of the Imperfect
given under the preceding sections is the *potential* or
permissive sense which it appears sometimes to convey.
It would, perhaps, be incorrect to say that the Imperfect
in itself possesses a potential or permissive sense; the fact
rather is that certain actions which we in English distinctly
state to be practicable or permissible, and the reverse,
the Hebrew represents merely as likely to take place or
customary, and the reverse.   Thus in a sentence referring
to past time we read,

וְהַמֶּלֶךְ שְׁלֹמֹה וְכָל־עֲדַת יִשְׂרָאֵל......מְזַבְּחִים צֹאן

וּבָקָר אֲשֶׁר לֹא־יִסָּפְרוּ וְלֹא יִמָּנוּ מֵרֹב׃

And King Solomon and all the congregation of Israel......were sacrificing sheep and oxen which could not be counted nor numbered for multitude (1 Kings viii. 5)

[In this instance, whereas the English idiom states the impossibility of counting the sacrifices, the Hebrew merely affirms that such a counting was not to take place.]

Similarly we find,

הַשָּׁמַיִם וּשְׁמֵי הַשָּׁמַיִם לֹא יְכַלְכְּלוּךָ

The heavens, yea the heavens of heavens, cannot contain Thee
(1 Kings viii. 27)

[In this sentence the words לֹא יְכַלְכְּלוּךָ do not state the *impossibility* of the heavens containing God (which would be expressed by לֹא יָכְלוּ לְכַלְכֵּל), but merely the fact that they do not habitually, and there is no likelihood that they will, contain Him.]

So likewise

לֹא־יֵעָשֶׂה כֵן

It ought not so to be done (Gen. xxix. 26)

[In this sentence the Hebrew merely states that a certain thing is contrary to custom, and therefore, since among the Hebrews law and custom are almost identical, contrary to law or right.]

V. The Imperfect, since it expresses what is customary, may be used to express some attribute or customary action qualifying

(a) a noun : e.g.

מִי אַתְּ וַתִּירְאִי מֵאֱנוֹשׁ יָמוּת וּמִבֶּן־אָדָם חָצִיר יִנָּתֵן

*Who art thou that thou shouldest have been afraid of a
mortal man that dies, or of a human being that is made
(like) grass ?* (Isaiah li. 12)

כַּכַּלָּה תַּעְדֶּה כֵלֶיהָ

As a bride who adorns herself with her (bridal) attire
(Isaiah lxi. 10)

(b) a verb, whether it be

(α) a Perfect : e.g.

הֶחֱשֵׁיתִי מֵעוֹלָם אַחֲרִישׁ אֶתְאַפָּק

*I have long been silent, holding my peace, refraining
myself* (Isaiah xlii. 14)

אַתְּ נָטַשְׁתְּ אֹתִי......אָחוֹר תֵּלֵכִי

Thou hast forsaken me......going backward (Jerem. xv. 6)

(β) an Imperfect with Wāw consecutive : e.g.

וַיֵּצֵא דָוִד בְּכֹל אֲשֶׁר יִשְׁלָחֶנּוּ שָׁאוּל יַשְׂכִּיל

*And David went forth whithersoever Saul used to send
him, doing prudently* (1 Sam. xviii. 5)

וַיֵּצֵא הַמַּשְׁחִית מִמַּחֲנֵה פְלִשְׁתִּים שְׁלֹשָׁה רָאשִׁים
הָרֹאשׁ אֶחָד יִפְנֶה וגו'

*And the raiders went out from the camp of the Philistines
in three companies, the one company turning, etc.*
(1 Sam. xiii. 17)[1]

---

[1] In the last two illustrations it is possible that in each case the
pointing should be וַיֵּצְאוּ ; but this would not affect the explanation of
the Imperfect, which in any case merely qualifies and describes the
action of the main verb.

(γ)   an Imperfect referring to future time : e.g.

אִם־תֵּלֵךְ לְפָנַי......חֻקַּי וּמִשְׁפָּטַי תִּשְׁמֹר

If thou wilt walk before me......keeping my statutes
and my ordinances (1 Kings ix. 4)

אָשׁוּבָה אֶרְעֶה צֹאנְךָ אֶשְׁמֹר

I will again shepherd thy flock, keeping guard
(Gen. xxx. 31)

[In this sentence אֶשְׁמֹר is used to qualify the previous

אֶרְעֶה, and אָשׁוּבָה : אֶרְעֶה, being in close connexion, are
construed ἀσυνδέτως.]

(δ)   or a Participle : e.g.

הוֹי מַשְׁכִּימֵי בַבֹּקֶר שֵׁכָר יִרְדֹּפוּ

Ho! you who are early in the morning, following[1]
after strong drink (Isaiah v. 11)

מֵקִים מֵעָפָר דָּל מֵאַשְׁפֹּת יָרִים אֶבְיוֹן

He raises up from the ground the poor, lifting up the
needy from the ash heap (1 Sam. ii. 8)

VI.   Since the action contemplated as future frequently depends upon the will of the speaker, the
Imperfect is naturally often used in commands : e.g.

מוֹצָא שְׂפָתֶיךָ תִּשְׁמֹר וְעָשִׂיתָ

That which thy lips utter thou shalt keep and do
(Deut. xxiii. 24)

---

[1] The *third* person is constantly used in Hebrew as in Syriac to
qualify a noun in the vocative.

לֹא תַחְמֹד

Thou shalt not covet (Ex. xx. 17)

גַּם־לִי גַם־לָךְ לֹא יִהְיֶה

It shall be neither mine nor thine (1 Kings iii. 26)

VII. The Imperfect is used to express actions which in Latin would be expressed by the Subjunctive mood[1], when the idea is the development of the action, both

(a) in the future: e.g.

הַרְבִּי שִׁיר לְמַעַן תִּזָּכֵרִי

Sing many songs that thou mayest be remembered
(Isaiah xxiii. 16)

---

[1] In such sentences as מִי אָנֹכִי כִּי אֵלֵךְ *Who am I, that I should go?* (Ex. iii. 11), מָה אֱנוֹשׁ כִּי תִזְכְּרֶנּוּ *What is man that thou art mindful of him?* (Ps. viii. 5) the Imperfect does not, strictly speaking, correspond to a Subjunctive for כִּי is not a final particle. The exact structure of the sentence is easily seen, if for the interrogative pronoun a definite predicate be substituted; thus, *I am honoured*, **for** *I shall go*; *Man is great*, **for** *thou art mindful of him*. That this is the true explanation is shewn by such sentences as 1 Kings xviii. 9, 2 Kings v. 7, where כִּי is followed by a Participle, and 2 Sam. vii. 18, where it is followed by a Perfect. Similarly in the sentence לֹא אִישׁ אֵל וִיכַזֵּב *God is not a man that He should lie* (Num. xxiii. 19), the Imperfect does not represent a Subjunctive. The exact meaning of the sentence is, *It is not the case that God is a man and so wont to lie.* A similar use of the Imperfect, but without the conjunction, occurs in יהוה רֹעִי לֹא אֶחְסָר *Jehovah is my shepherd, therefore shall I lack nothing* (Ps. xxiii. 1). So also לֹא מְשַׂנְאִי עָלַי הִגְדִּיל וְאֶסָּתֵר (Ps. lv. 13) means *It is not the case that my enemy has done great things against me and I shall therefore hide myself from him.* This construction however is rare, and in the last example the sense would be expressed in prose by כִּי עַתָּה followed by the Perfect; cf. 1 Sam. xiii. 13. The chief objection to the explanation here given is that it involves a simple Imperfect with weak Wāw. But this construction though not common certainly occurs in the Hebrew Bible; see below, Exceptions to the rule of Wāw Consecutive.

וְעַתָּה פֶּן־יִשְׁלַח יָדוֹ וגו׳

And now lest he put forth his hand, etc. (Gen. iii. 22)

and

(b) in the past : e.g.

לְמַעַן יֵדְעוּ דּוֹר אַחֲרוֹן בָּנִים יִוָּלֵדוּ

*In order that a later generation, children (yet) to
be born, might know* (Ps lxxviii. 6)

פֶּן־תֹּאמַר הִנֵּה יְדַעְתִּין

Lest thou shouldest say, Behold I knew them
(Isaiah xlviii. 7)

[In this latter case (b) the Infinitive is more usual.]

N.B. The Imperfect in the sense of a Subjunctive
sometimes follows another tense, whether Perfect or
Imperfect, without any subordinating particle : e.g. יהוה
חָפֵץ לְמַעַן צִדְקוֹ יַגְדִּיל תּוֹרָה וְיַאְדִּיר *Jehovah was pleased
for His righteousness' sake to make a tôrah great and
glorious* (Isaiah xlii. 21): לֹא תוֹסִיפִי יִקְרְאוּ לָךְ *They shall
not call thee again* [i.e. thou shalt not enjoy again—
literally, thou shalt not add—the state which may be
described by the words יִקְרְאוּ לָךְ] (Isaiah xlvii. 1).

VIII. The Imperfect is naturally used in hypothetical sentences, when the idea to be expressed is that
of an incomplete action :

(a) with a hypothetical particle : e.g.

אִם־לֹא תֵלְכִי עִמִּי לֹא אֵלֵךְ

If thou wilt not go with me, I will not go (Judges iv. 8)

2—2

[This use is identical with that by which the Imperfect expresses a simple Future.]

(b)   without a hypothetical particle : e.g.

הִנֵּה תִרְאוּ אִישׁ מִשְׁתַּגֵּעַ לָמָּה תָבִיאוּ אֹתוֹ אֵלָי

Lo, if you see somebody raving, why should you bring him to me ? (1 Sam. xxi. 15)

הָאִישׁ אֶחָד יֶחֱטָא וְעַל־כָּל־הָעֵדָה תִּקְצֹף

If only one man sin, wilt thou be angry with the whole congregation ? (Num. xvi. 22)

וְהִנֵּה נֵלֵךְ וּמַה־נָּבִיא לָאִישׁ

And lo, if we go, what shall we take to the man ? (1 Sam. ix. 7)

N.B.   This use of the Imperfect is analogous to that of the Perfect described in § x. In this case the first clause is not subordinate but coordinate[1].

---

[1] Here belong such sentences as Ps. cxlvi. 4 *a*.

THE COHORTATIVE, JUSSIVE, AND IMPERATIVE.

In addition to the ordinary form of the Imperfect two modifications of it are commonly found in Hebrew, known severally as the Cohortative and the Jussive. As the names imply, both these modifications are used to denote actions as willed or intended. The Cohortative is confined almost exclusively to the first person, singular and plural, while the Jussive is scarcely ever found except in the second and third persons, singular and plural. These two forms of the Imperfect are therefore supplementary to one another.

The Cohortative is easily recognised by the ending הָ־[1] (e.g. אֶקְטְלָה, נִקְטְלָה, which become in pause נִקְטָלָה, אֶקְטָלָה), except in ל״ה verbs, in which forms that are obviously used in the sense of the Cohortative have nevertheless the pointing of the ordinary Imperfect[2].

---

[1] This הָ־ appears to be identical in origin with the an of the Arabic Energetic. It is possible that in several of the cases in which we find the so-called 'epenthetic nun' before suffixes we have actually the Cohortative in its old form. See, for example, 2 Kings vi. 28, 29, where וְנֹאכְלֶנּוּ is equivalent to וְנֹאכְלָה אֹתוֹ, whereas on the other hand וַנֹּאכְלֵהוּ (v. 29) is equivalent to וַנֹּאכַל אֹתוֹ. Ordinarily, however, the Cohortative with suffixes is identical in form with the Imperfect.

[2] The only exceptions are וְנִשְׁתָּעָה (Isaiah xli. 23) and וְאֶשְׁעָה (Ps. cxix. 117). It is, however, doubtful whether with so few examples we are justified in assuming that ל״ה verbs could take the ending הָ־ in the Cohortative. In both words quoted above the ending הָ־ may have been

The Jussive is in the majority of instances identical in form with the Imperfect[1], and differs from it only in two cases, (*a*) when the vowel before the last radical of the Imperfect is essentially long (as in the Hiph'îl of the strong verbs, and in the Ḳal, Niph'al, and Hiph'îl of ע"ו verbs), in which case the Jussive appears with the corresponding tone-long or heightened vowel, (*b*) when the Imperfect ends in הָ֖ (i.e. in forms derived from the so-called ל"ה verbs), in which case the corresponding Jussive form drops the final הָ֖.

Both the Cohortative and Jussive denote actions as willed by the speaker.

I.   Thus the Cohortative expresses a desire,

(*a*)   when the gratification of the desire is in the power of the speaker or speakers: e.g.

אָסֻרָה־נָּא

I will turn aside (Ex. iii. 3)

---

adopted by the punctuators simply for the purpose of securing assonance with the preceding Cohortatives. That the Masoretes did not scruple arbitrarily to alter the pronunciation for the sake of assonance is clear from such passages as 1 Kings xvii. 14, where תִּכְלָה is so pointed for the sake of assonance with תֶּחְסָר: cf. מבואך (2 Sam. iii. 25) altered in Ḳ'rî into מוֹבָאֶךָ for assonance with the preceding מוֹצָאֶךָ. At the same time it is not impossible that all Cohortatives from ל"ה verbs should be pointed with Ḳameṣ, an obsolete form having been ignored by the later tradition.

[1] This is always the case when the Jussive has suffixes attached to it. There are two exceptions according to the Masoretic pointing, viz. וְיַגֵּדְךָ (Deut. xxxii. 7) and וְיֹשֵׁעֲכֶם (Isaiah xxxv. 4). It is difficult however in the face of the frequent glaring inconsistencies in the Masoretic pointing to attach much importance to these exceptions. Probably the words should be pointed וְיַגֶּדְךָ and וְיֹשַׁעֲכֶם.

אֲנִי וְהַנַּעַר נֵלְכָה

The lad and I will go (Gen. xxii. 5)

(*b*) when it depends upon the permission or will of another: e.g.

אִם־מָצָאתִי חֵן בְּעֵינֶיךָ אִמָּלְטָה נָּא

If I have found favour in thy sight, let me slip away
(1 Sam. xx. 29)

אָנָּה יהוה אַל־נָא נֹאבְדָה בְּנֶפֶשׁ הָאִישׁ הַזֶּה

O Jehovah! let us not perish for the life of this man
(Jonah i. 14)

(*c*) when the speaker desires that others should act with himself: e.g.

נֵרְדָה

Let us go down (Gen. xi. 7)

לְכוּ נְרַנְּנָה לַיהוה

Come, let us shout for joy to Jehovah (Ps. xcv. 1)

II. Similarly the Jussive expresses a desire when the gratification of it is

(*a*) in the speaker's own power, i.e. a command: e.g.

יְהִי אוֹר

Let there be light (Gen. i. 3)

אִישׁ אַל־יוֹתֵר מִמֶּנּוּ עַד־הַבֹּקֶר

Let no one leave of it till the morning (Ex. xvi. 19)

(*b*) dependent upon the will of others: e.g.

יֵרֶא פַרְעֹה אִישׁ

Let Pharaoh select a man (Gen. xli. 33)

יְחִי הַמֶּלֶךְ שְׁלֹמֹה

Long live King Solomon (1 Kings i. 39)

III. It will thus be seen that the Jussive resembles the Imperative in meaning, and practically supplies it with the third person which is lacking. This being the case, it is not surprising that the second person of the Jussive is very rare except with the negative אַל[1], that is, as a rule, it only takes the place of the Imperative when the latter on account of the negative cannot be used.

There are therefore in Hebrew three verbal forms expressing desire (each possessing various modifications of intensity), viz. (1) the Cohortative, belonging chiefly to the first person[2]; (2) the Imperative, belonging to the second person; (3) the Jussive, belonging chiefly to the second and third persons[3]. These three verbal forms are so exactly similar in meaning, that in treating of their idiomatic use it will be convenient to take them together.

IV. We have already noticed the decided preference shewn by the Hebrew for coordination rather than subordination. In many cases where the English idiom

---

[1] According to the Masoretic pointing תּוֹחֵל (1 Sam. x. 8) is a Jussive used in a positive command, but probably the form should be pointed as an Imperfect. See below.

[2] But also to the second person, e.g. תָעֻפָה (Job xi. 17), and to the third, e.g. וְתָבוֹאֶה, יַחִישָׁה (Isaiah v. 19).

[3] But also to the first, e.g. וְאֶכְתֹּב (Deut. x. 2), וְנֵרֶא (Isaiah xli. 23 K'thîbh).

would subordinate a clause, the Hebrew simply coupled together by *wāw* two or more coordinate clauses, and looked to the result of the whole. Thus, for example, the two coordinate clauses לֹא יִבְנוּ וְאַחֵר יֵשֵׁב (Isaiah lxv. 22) mean, 'It will not be the case that, *when they shall build*, another shall inhabit'; in other words the לֹא at the head of the sentence negatives *the result expressed by the two coordinate clauses* יִבְנוּ וְאַחֵר יֵשֵׁב.

When therefore a certain desired result is expressed in Hebrew by two coordinate tenses (Cohortative, Imperative, or Jussive), coupled together by simple *wāw*, the sense will be that which is obtained in English by subordinating a clause.

The following are illustrations of this idiom:

(a)   two Cohortatives: e.g.

אָרוּצָה נָּא וַאֲבַשְּׂרָה אֶת־הַמֶּלֶךְ

Let me run, that I may take tidings to the king
(2 Sam. xviii. 19)

[In this sentence both verbs are coordinate, the end chiefly desired being expressed by the latter verb[1]. It happens that in this particular case English colloquial

---

[1] It may indeed be stated as a general rule that, when two parallel clauses occur, the emphasis is on the second; so that in an English rendering of two such *indicative* clauses the first may frequently be subordinated by some such word as 'whereas' or 'although': e.g. וְהָיָה רֵאשִׁיתְךָ מִצְעָר וְאַחֲרִיתְךָ יִשְׂגֶּה מְאֹד (Job viii. 7) *And it shall come to pass that, though thy beginning were small, thy latter end shall become very great*; cf. S. Matt. xi. 25, Rom. vi. 17, 1 S. Pet. iv. 6.

idiom allows of a literal translation, 'Let me run and take' etc. Perhaps the rendering which would best bring out the exact meaning of the Hebrew sentence would be 'Let me by running take' etc.]

(*b*)   an Imperative followed by a Cohortative: e.g.

לְכָה אֵלַי וְאֶתְּנָה אֶת־בְּשָׂרְךָ לְעוֹף הַשָּׁמָיִם

Come to me, that I may give thy flesh to the birds of the air (1 Sam. xvii. 44)

(*c*)   a Jussive followed by a Cohortative: e.g.

וְתִקְרַב וְתָבוֹאָה עֲצַת קְדוֹשׁ יִשְׂרָאֵל וְנֵדָעָה

And let the purpose of the Holy One of Israel draw nigh and come, that we may know (Isaiah v. 19)

(*d*)   a Cohortative followed by an Imperative: e.g.

לְכִי אִיעָצֵךְ נָא עֵצָה וּמַלְּטִי אֶת־נַפְשֵׁךְ

Come, let me advise thee, that thou mayest save thy life (1 Kings i. 12)

(*e*)   a Cohortative followed by a Jussive: e.g.

לְכוּ וְנַעֲלֶה אֶל־הַר יהוה......וְיוֹרֵנוּ מִדְּרָכָיו

Come and let us go up to the mountain of Jehovah...... that He may teach us of His ways (Isaiah ii. 3)

(*f*)   two Imperatives: e.g.

זֹאת עֲשׂוּ וִחְיוּ

Do this, that ye may live (Gen. xlii. 18)

(*g*) an Imperative followed by a Jussive: e.g.

שִׁמְעוּ וּתְחִי נַפְשְׁכֶם

Hear, that your soul may live (Isaiah lv. 3)

(*h*) two Jussives : e.g.

יֵלְכוּ־נָא וִיבַקְשׁוּ אֶת־אֲדֹנֶיךָ

Let them go, that they may seek thy master (2 Kings ii. 16)

V. A somewhat similar use of the Cohortative and the Jussive is sometimes found,

(*a*) after a question implying a wish : e.g.

הַאֵין פֹּה נָבִיא לַיהוה עוֹד וְנִדְרְשָׁה מֵאוֹתוֹ

Is there not here another prophet of Jehovah's (implying ' I wish there were here another prophet '), *that we may inquire of him ?* (1 Kings xxii. 7)

מִי יְפַתֶּה אֶת־אַחְאָב וְיַעַל

Who will entice Ahab (= I want someone to entice Ahab) *that he may go up ?* (1 Kings xxii. 20)

(*b*) after a statement of which the logical sequence is the expression of a wish : e.g.

וּנְבִיאֵי הַבַּעַל אַרְבַּע מֵאוֹת וַחֲמִשִּׁים אִישׁ וְיִתְּנוּ לָנוּ וגו'

But the prophets of Baal are four hundred and fifty men ; and so let them give, etc. (1 Kings xviii. 22, 23)

[In this sentence the statement of the numerical superiority of the prophets of Baal suggests the wish that they may prove by a sign their spiritual superiority.]

אוּלַי יְפֻתֶּה וְנוּכְלָה לוֹ

Perhaps he will be enticed, so that we may prevail over him (Jerem. xx. 10)

אוּלַי יָשֵׁן הוּא וְיָקָץ

Perhaps he is asleep so that he must be awoke
(1 Kings xviii. 27)

(*c*) after a direct negative, when the logical sequence of the corresponding positive statement would be the expression of a wish: e.g.

וְאֵין יוֹעֵץ וְאֶשְׁאָלֵם וְיָשִׁיבוּ דָבָר

And there are no counsellors so that, when I ask them, they may answer (Isaiah xli. 28)

[The exact force of this sentence may be seen by changing the negative into a positive statement, viz. 'There are counsellors, and so I will ask them.' See above, § IV., and also on the Imperfect § VII., footnote.]

לֹא תַחְפֹּץ זֶבַח וְאֶתֵּנָה

Thou wilt not have me give sacrifice[1] (Ps. li. 18)

---

[1] Occasionally in such sentences the conjunction is omitted: e.g.
לֹא יֵשׁ בֵּינֵינוּ מוֹכִיחַ יָשֵׁת יָדוֹ עַל־שְׁנֵינוּ *There is no arbiter between us, to lay his hand upon us both* (Job ix. 33); but perhaps in this case we should point לֹא after the analogy of Num. xxii. 29, Job xvi. 4. Cf. the omission of the conjunction before an *Imperfect denoting the result* of a statement, e.g. יהוה רֹעִי לֹא אֶחְסָר (Ps. xxiii. 1).

N.B. When in sentences similar to those that are treated of in § IV. it is necessary to negative the second verb, the Hebrew does not use the Cohortative or Jussive with אַל, but the simple Imperfect with לֹא[1]. In other words it states the *negative consequence* of the desire expressed in the first clause, rather that the *negative purpose*: e.g. רֵד וְלֹא יַעְצָרְכָה הַגָּשֶׁם *Go down, that the rain may not stop thee* (literally *and the rain will not stop thee*) (1 Kings xviii. 44): אַל־תַּעֲלוּ......וְלֹא תִנָּגְפוּ *Go not up......that ye may not be smitten* (literally *and ye will not be smitten*) (Num. xiv. 42). When וְאַל is found followed by a Jussive, it negatives a distinct desire co-ordinate with the former one or synonymous with it: e.g. נִירוּ לָכֶם נִיר וְאַל־תִּזְרְעוּ אֶל־קֹצִים *Plough up for your-selves ploughland, and scatter not your seed among thorns* (Jeremiah iv. 3): אַל־תִּשְׁלַח יָדְךָ אֶל־הַנַּעַר וְאַל־תַּעַשׂ לוֹ מְאוּמָה *Stretch not out thine hand against the lad, and do not unto him anything* (Gen. xxii. 12): אַל־תִּירְאוּ וְאַל־תַּעַרְצוּ מִפְּנֵיהֶם *Be not afraid, and be not terrified because of them* (Deut. xxxi. 6).

---

[1] There are some instances in which according to the Masoretic pointing the Jussive stands after לֹא, but as they are very few in number, and as two of them, viz. 1 Sam. xiv. 36, 2 Sam. xvii. 12, involve the additional peculiarity of the first person plural Jussive, it is probable that in every case the pointing of the Imperfect should be adopted.

ADDITIONAL NOTES ON THE COHORTATIVE AND THE JUSSIVE.

I. In some of the examples given under § IV. the sense would not be very different if a hypothetical form were adopted: e.g. זֹאת עֲשֹׂוּ וִחְיוּ *Do this, that ye may live* does not greatly differ in meaning from the sentence expressed hypothetically, *If ye do this, ye shall live*; and sentences of this type frequently occur in Hebrew where a hypothetical form may be adopted in an English translation. At the same time such a sentence does not, as a rule, denote a *mere hypothesis,* but there is the *actual expression of a wish,* whether real, as in the sentence זֹאת עֲשֹׂוּ וִחְיוּ, or ironical, as in עֻצוּ עֵצָה וְתֻפָר *Take ye counsel, that it may come to nought!* (Isaiah viii. 10).

There are however some passages in which two Jussives or Cohortatives appear to express a mere hypothesis. Of these the stock illustration is תָּשֶׁת חֹשֶׁךְ וִיהִי לָיְלָה (Ps. civ. 20), which seems to mean *When thou makest darkness, night comes on.* Other examples are,

אַל־יוֹשִׁעֵךְ יְהוָֹה מֵאַיִן אוֹשִׁיעֵךְ

If Jehovah will not help thee, whence am I to help thee?
(2 Kings vi. 27)

אוֹדְךָ יְהוָֹה כִּי אָנַפְתָּ בִּי יָשֹׁב אַפְּךָ וּתְנַחֲמֵנִי

I will thank Thee, O Jehovah, that, though Thou mayest have been angry with me, when Thine anger turneth away, then Thou comfortest me (Isaiah xii. 1)

יַךְ וְיַחְבְּשֵׁנוּ

When He smites, He binds us up (Hosea vi. 1)

There are several other passages which might be quoted under this head, but either they are such as may be explained as having an ironical sense, or they may be considered as Imperfects, according to the use of the Imperfect described in § VIII. (*b*). It is therefore necessary to inquire whether the passages just quoted are rightly understood as hypothetical. As to Isaiah xii. 1 it must be confessed that the text as it stands is awkward. A simple correction would be to insert a *wāw* before יָשׁב, pointing both it and the *wāw* of the following verb as Wāw Consecutive, in which case the sentence would mean *I will thank Thee, O Jehovah, that though Thou hast been angry with me* (literally 'that Thou hast been angry with me, and,' see remarks on Coordination, § IV. preceding,) *Thine anger is turned away, and Thou hast comforted me.* The text of Hosea is far from certain, and it is possible that in vi. 1 we should read יַךְ וְיַחְבְּשֵׁנוּ. The interpretation of 2 Kings vi. 27 depends upon the punctuation of the passage, and by disregarding the Masoretic tradition we may translate, *Nay! let Jehovah save thee; whence am I to save thee?*[1] There remains Ps. civ. 20, and here we are at once struck by the fact that, according to the vowel points, תָּשֶׁת is the second person of the Jussive, which, with the exception of some doubtful instances, is only used after אַל, the Imperative taking its place. Moreover, as Professor Driver

---

[1] At the same time it must be admitted that the use of אַל without a verb is not common, though it occurs in Gen. xxxiii. 10, 2 Sam. xiii. 25, 2 Kings iii. 13, Ruth i. 13. In the present instance moreover there is no verb which is naturally supplied by the context. We should expect to find אַל־תִּצְעֲקִי אֵלַי *cry not unto me.* Perhaps the real solution of the difficulty is to read אֵלֶיהָ יוֹשִׁיעֵךְ *unto her, Let Jehovah save thee,* etc.

has pointed out, the tenses employed in other verses of the same psalm, e.g. *v.* 17, are *Imperfects*, as is clear from their *Indicative* force. It seems therefore not improbable that we should point תֵּשֵׁת, and correct וִיהִי into וַיְהִי or וְהָיָה.

In any case considering the small number of instances in which, according to the Masoretic text, it is necessary to understand two Jussives as expressing a mere hypothesis, and having regard to the uncertainty as to the text in some of these instances, it will be safest to consider this usage of the Jussive as not proven.

II. There are a few instances in which the Jussive with simple *wāw* appears to be used in order to express a purpose after a Perfect referring to past time. It may be that the original force of the Jussive was forgotten and that it had crystallized into a *final* sense, or that, as the Imperfect might be used to express an action future from some standpoint in the past, so the Jussive could be used to express a wish from a standpoint in the past.

The number of passages however in which this is apparently the case is very small, and in some of them we may point the verb with Wāw Consecutive. Thus, to consider some of the passages quoted by Professor Driver in this connexion, in 1 Kings xiii. 33 it is possible to point, with the Septuagint, וַיְהִי. So also in 2 Kings xix. 25 וַתְּהִי (with Wāw Consecutive) is more natural after the Perfect הֲבֵיאתִיהָ *I have brought it about.* Similarly in Isaiah xxv. 9 we may point וְיוֹשִׁיעֵנוּ *and He has saved us.* In Ps. xlix. 10 the Jussive וִיהִי does not seem to carry on the sense expressed by any Perfect, and the text of this psalm is not above suspicion. In Ps. lxxxi. 16 the psalmist is expressing a hope for the future[1], so that there is

---

[1] Perhaps in *v.* 14 of this psalm we ought to point שְׁמַע, i.e. as an Imperative. לוּ followed by an Imperative occurs in Gen. xxiii. 13, and

nothing anomalous in the use of the Jussive. In 2 Chron.
xxiv. 11 the *Imperfect* sense is more natural than the
Jussive, though such a construction would not have been
employed in the Hebrew of the golden age. The remaining
passages quoted by Professor Driver are Lam. i. 19 and
2 Chron. xxiii. 19. In the latter passage the use of לֹא
shews that we have an Imperfect (see note to the sections
treating of the final sense of the Cohortative and Jussive),
and Lam. i. 19 is hardly sufficient in itself to establish
a meaning of the Jussive which seems opposed to its
fundamental sense. Perhaps, if the text be correct we
may understand וַיָּשִׁיבוּ as an Imperfect according to the
usage of the Imperfect described in § II.[1] In Isaiah
xli. 26 וְנֵדָעָה and וְנֹאמַר may be translated *that we may
recognize* and *that we may say*: i.e. the sentence is virtually
a conditional one, 'if there is any one who has declared
these events beforehand, we for our part are ready to say'
etc.

III.   There are some instances in which Cohortatives
and Jussives are used apparently with the sense of simple
Imperfects, e.g. אוֹחִילָה (Jeremiah iv. 19 *K'rî*), אֶשְׁמָעָה

---

it is to be noticed that *vv.* 5, 14 end with the unusual expression לֵאמֹר לוֹ
while in *vv.* 6, 15 the first verb is in each case an Imperative. Probably
we should point לוֹ in each case, attaching the word to the following
verse, and reading לְ‍אַ for לֹא in *v.* 11.

[1] Cf. וְאֶעֱלִים 1 Sam. xii. 3. In this passage however the text is very
uncertain (see LXX), and the pointing וְאַעֲלִים would certainly be
possible. The Masoretes however seem to have considered that an
Imperfect or Jussive with weak *wāw* might represent a purpose after a
Perfect. The Targum paraphrase of Jeremiah v. 28 seems to imply a
translation 'They have not judged......in order that they may prosper.'
It is noteworthy that in 2 Chron. xxiii. 19, though יָבוֹא is Imperfect, the
Chronicler has used after a past tense the same construction as would be
used after a present or future.

(ib. 21), אֲפוּנָה (Ps. lxxxviii. 16), וְתָעַל (Joel ii. 20), אָחוּ
(Job xxiii. 9), אָט (ib. 11), etc. Assuming that the text
is correct in such places, the only possible explanation
appears to be that the Cohortative and Jussive forms
have lost their meaning, and are merely used poetically.
In the case of the latest portions of the Old Testament
there would not be a great difficulty in adopting this
explanation, for some of the latest psalms are remarkable
for their use of archaic endings which have entirely lost
their significance, but it is difficult to suppose that this
could have been the case in the time of the prophet
Jeremiah. Upon the whole, considering the paucity of
instances in which it is necessary to suppose that these
forms have lost their meaning, and the unsatisfactory
state of the text of the Old Testament, it is at least not
improbable that the text is in error, especially as the
apparent deviations from the rule occur sporadically and
cannot be shewn to belong to the idiosyncrasy of any
particular author. A study of the spelling of the Masoretic
text leads one to the conviction that in a great number
of cases final vowels were still in use which were not
commonly represented by vowel letters. Thus when the
suffix of the 3rd person sing. masc. is represented by a ה,
it is natural to suppose that it was intended originally
that it should be pronounced with a final vowel[1]; cf. forms
like רֵעֵהוּ, מִינְהוּ. This supposition is greatly confirmed
by an examination of the pointing of הִנֵּה *behold*. Leaving
out of account doubtful cases there are about twenty
passages in which הִנֵּה is immediately followed by a
predicate other than a finite verb. On the other hand
there are some ten passages in which הִנֵּה is followed by a
pronoun of the third person singular or plural. הִנּוֹ occurs

---

[1] That the Masoretes were uncertain whether the spelling with ה in
such cases was a justifiable variation of the spelling with ו is seen from
the fact that in some places, e.g. Gen. xlix. 11, a *K'ri* is added.

three times, הִנֵּנוּ once (in Ḳ'thîbh), הִנָּם thirty-seven times. הִנָּה never occurs. The form הֵן is never used except where the nominative is actually expressed, and הִנֵּה is never found followed by a plural participle or adjective without a nominative. In the light of these facts we can hardly doubt that in many cases הנה was meant to be pronounced הִנֵּנוּ or, if feminine, הִנֵּה. It is at least remarkable that while the Masoretic text gives us הִנֵּה כְתוּבָה (2 Sam. i. 18) we never find הִנֵּה כְתוּבִים but always הִנָּם כְּתוּבִים. Similarly, as Professor Driver has shewn in his Commentary on Deuteronomy, pp. 78, 79, it is probable that אֵל *these* was originally intended to be pronounced with a final vowel viz. אֵלֶּה. On the other hand the so-called *wāw* and *yōdh compaginis*, if, as seems most probable, they are in reality merely case-endings that have lost their meaning, may possibly represent final vowels which were commonly *pronounced* though, being short, they were not commonly *written*. If this supposition be correct the fact that they occur most frequently in the latest portions of the Old Testament is readily explained by the late origin of the *scriptio plena*.

Moreover it must be remembered that the grammar of the Old Testament is practically the same throughout, a fact which is very significant when we remember that the literature of the Old Testament extends over a period of scarcely less than a thousand years. In such a space of time the grammar would inevitably become modified, especially when from the almost vowelless character of the writing, modification would be in many cases imperceptibly introduced. Sometimes indeed we have words which point to grammatical forms different from those in use left through a misconception of their meaning; e.g. שַׁקַּמְתִּי Judges v. 7, שַׁבַּרְתִּי and נְתַקְתִּי Jeremiah ii. 20 (cf. iii. 4,

3—2

5), וְהַחֲרִמֹתִי Micah iv. 13, when the 2nd person singular feminine Perfect is intended, and the *yôdh* has probably been allowed to remain, because it was mistaken in each case for the ending of the 1st person singular. So also in וַיִּשַׁנּוֹ 1 Sam. xxi. 14 and וַיַּכּוּ 2 Sam. xiv. 6 we have probably an archaic form of the Pi‘el Imperfect in *u* which has elsewhere been changed into הוּ֖ , but has been allowed to remain here, because it was supposed to be the suffix of the 3rd person masculine singular. This same form of the Pi‘el occurs on the Moabite Stone, viz. וַיְעַנּוֹ line 5, and אֲעַנּוֹ line 6.

Furthermore it must be remembered that the received Masoretic text seems to have been made up from a considerable number of manuscripts of various dates, and therefore of different modes of spelling, and that the vowels were not added till Hebrew had ceased to be a spoken language, and its place had been taken by Aramaic even in the Schools. In the latter language also there were considerable variations in spelling: e.g. in the Biblical Aramaic it is scarcely possible to decide as to the relative values of *ḥîreḳ* and *ṣêrê*. Under these circumstances the wonder is, not that there should be so many anomalies in the pointing of the Hebrew Bible, but that there should be so few.

These considerations may help us on the one hand to understand why in several instances we find forms pointed as Jussives when the grammar requires Imperfects, e.g. נִשְׁאַר 1 Sam. xiv. 36, which as the לֹא before it shews must be an Imperfect and should be pointed נִשָּׁאֵר (compare the precisely similar sentence 1 Kings xviii. 5 where the Imperfect is actually found וְלוֹא נַכְרִית), אָחַז Job xxiii. 9, which should be pointed אֶחֱזֶה (cf. אֶרְאֶה at the end of the same verse); and on the other hand we need not be surprised if a Cohortative is occasionally accidentally written for an Imperfect, especially when we find that the text of the passage in which it occurs exhibits signs of corruption.

Although we may freely acknowledge the enormous debt which we owe to the Masoretes, we may fairly hesitate to accept them as our guides in all matters of grammar. Seeing that in the overwhelming majority of cases, grammatical forms have a definite and easily recognized meaning, in the few instances where we find apparently a departure from the usual significance, it is at least as natural to suppose a corruption in the text, as it is to assume that a grammatical form, which ninety-nine times out of a hundred has a definite meaning, should the hundredth time lose this meaning altogether.

SEQUENCE OF TENSES.

The Imperfect with Wāw Consecutive.

I. We have seen that the Hebrew tenses convey no idea of time, but express merely the state of an action, and also that there is a marked preference for coordinate rather than subordinate clauses. It might therefore happen that we should occasionally be in doubt as to the *time* to be assigned to each of a number of actions—that is to say whether such actions should be understood as taking place simultaneously or successively—were it not that by an idiom peculiar to itself the Hebrew makes this perfectly clear. Thus in describing a series of actions in the past the Hebrew represents each successive action after the first as arising out of, or at least following upon, the one preceding. Thus in such a sentence as '*The Aramœans went out on forays and took captive etc.*,' it is clear that the second action is developed after, even if it is not the direct consequence of, the former action. Now the tense which expresses development is the Imperfect. It is therefore quite natural that the second action should be expressed by the Imperfect. In the case of the first action, however, it is unnecessary to represent it as developed out of some other action, for no such action is mentioned; and as a past action is usually thought of as

complete (unless it be necessary to dwell upon its several
stages), it is naturally represented by a Perfect. We
have therefore a Perfect יָצָא (expressing the completion
of the act of going out) and an Imperfect יִשְׁבּוּ (expressing the development of the act of taking captive)
coupled together by 'and' וְ. But though the Imperfect
יִשְׁבּוּ in any case represents the act of taking captive as
in course of development, we require to know definitely
that it is developed out of, or at least in connexion with,
the act of going out; and this is accomplished by means
of a more emphatic form of the conjunction 'and.' This
conjunction which originally had the form *wa*[1] is found in
such cases in its original form somewhat intensified by
the doubling of the preformative letter of the Imperfect,
e.g. וַיִּשְׁבּוּ. This emphatic form of the conjunction serves
to denote the close connexion between the word with
which it is combined and the previous clause; and since
the Imperfect expresses development, the natural inference
is that the action denoted by the Imperfect is developed

---

[1] That the original form of the conjunction was *wa* is proved not only
by the comparison of Arabic and Syriac, but also from the Hebrew itself.
Thus when two or more words are in close connexion, more especially
when they fall into pairs, if the second word be accented on the first
syllable, the conjunction is pointed וָ. See for example the eight words
falling into four pairs in Gen. viii. 22, viz. זֶרַע וְקָצִיר, וְקֹר וָחֹם
וְקַיִץ וָחֹרֶף, וְיוֹם וָלַיְלָה.
The doubling of the preformative letter of the Imperfect arises
probably merely through the desire to keep the syllable *wa* clear and
distinct. It may be compared with the doubling of the מ in לָמָּה, which
before a guttural, especially when a ḥāṭēf vowel follows, appears in its
original form לָמָה.

out of, or after, the action denoted by the Perfect. This emphatic conjunction *wāw* is called Wāw Consecutive.

The old name 'Wāw Conversive,' which is a translation of the Hebrew וָו הַפּוּךְ, arose from the idea that the two tenses were respectively *Past* and *Future,* and that the 'Wāw Conversive' *converted* the one into the other; but it must be clearly understood that in this idiom the original meaning of the tense is not in any way changed by the *wāw*, which simply serves to connect it as closely as possible with the previous clause.

This emphatic syllable prefixed to the Imperfect has a tendency to modify the word by drawing back the tone. This can however take place only when the penultimate syllable[1] is open, and the word is out of pause. Thus we find וַיִּזְכֹּר, וַיִּקְרָא, וַיִּבָּתֵר[2], וַיִּשְׁלֶךְ, but from יֵלֵךְ we get וַיֵּצֶר יֵצֶר, from וַיֹּאמֶר יֹאמֶר, from וַיָּקָם יָקוּם, from וַיֵּלֶךְ, from וַיְבָרֶךְ יְבָרֵךְ, from וַיָּשֶׂם יָשִׂים. The tendency of this drawing back of the accent was to make the Imperfect in such cases resemble the Jussive, and accordingly in nearly all cases where the Jussive can be distinguished in form from the ordinary Imperfect we find the Imperfect with Wāw Consecutive assimilated to the form of the Jussive. It is probable indeed that the verbal form in such cases was actually regarded as the Jussive, and hence by a mistaken analogy the Cohortative was frequently used with Wāw Consecutive in the first person.

---

[1] The tone can never be drawn farther back than the last syllable but one. Words like הַבָּיְתָה are not real exceptions, for the *sh'wā* should by analogy be silent.

[2] The *dāghēsh* is always omitted with *yōdh* when it is followed by a *sh'wā*.

We see therefore that in describing a series of actions
in the past the Hebrew expresses the first action by the
Perfect, since it is thought of as complete, and each subsequent action by the Imperfect with Wāw Consecutive;
the emphatic form of the conjunction and the tense
denoting development together signifying that such
action is developed out of the one preceding: e.g.

וַאֲרָם יָצְאוּ גְדוּדִים וַיִּשְׁבּוּ מֵאֶרֶץ יִשְׂרָאֵל נַעֲרָה

קְטַנָּה וַתְּהִי לִפְנֵי אֵשֶׁת נַעֲמָן

Now the Aramæans went out on forays, and took captive from
the land of Israel a little maid, and she became the servant
of (lit. *was before*) *Naaman's wife* (2 Kings v. 2)

פַּרְעֹה מֶלֶךְ מִצְרַיִם עָלָה וַיִּלְכֹּד אֶת־גֶּזֶר וַיִּשְׂרְפָהּ בָּאֵשׁ

Pharaoh, king of Egypt, came up and took Gezer, and
burnt it with fire (1 Kings ix. 16)

N.B. Since Hebrew for the most part uses coordination rather than subordination, and the best Hebrew style
consists of short clauses coupled together by ו *and*[1], the
Imperfect with Wāw Consecutive is naturally the tense
most commonly employed in describing a series of actions

---

[1] It may perhaps be well to draw attention to the fact that the
Hebrew relates a history in the exact order of each action, and never
puts into a subordinate clause any portion of the main narrative. This
will be abundantly impressed upon the mind of anyone who attempts to
translate the Acts of the Apostles into Hebrew. Thus, for example,
in Acts xiv. 19 a Hebrew would never have expressed in a subordinate
clause so important a fact as the stoning of S. Paul. The verse in
Hebrew would rather run thus, 'And there came thither certain Jews
from Antioch and Iconium, **and** they persuaded the people, **and** they
stoned Paul, **and** drew him out of the city, for they supposed, etc.'

in the past[1]. It is however essential that the verb should
stand at the head of the 'consecutive' clause, for in a less
emphatic position the idea that the action of the Imperfect is developed out of that of the preceding clause is
overlooked. Accordingly in a negative sentence, since
the negative must always stand before the verb, the
construction with Wāw Consecutive is impossible. Thus
we find

$$\text{וַיְמַשֵּׁשׁ לָבָן אֶת־כָּל־הָאֹהֶל וְלֹא מָצָא}$$

And Laban searched all the tent, but did not find (them)
(Gen. xxxi. 34)

and likewise

$$\text{וַתֻּקַּח הָאִשָּׁה בֵּית פַּרְעֹה וּלְאַבְרָם הֵיטִיב בַּעֲבוּרָהּ}$$

And the woman was taken into Pharaoh's house, and Abram
(for his part) he (Pharaoh) treated well on her account
(Gen. xii. 15, 16)

[In this sentence it is desirable to contrast Abram
with Sarai, and for this reason וּלְאַבְרָם is put first in the
second clause, thereby making the construction with
Wāw Consecutive impossible in that clause.]

II. Although according to its precise meaning the
Imperfect with Wāw Consecutive expresses direct sequence in time, it has nevertheless become so common in
Hebrew, that it is sometimes used in a clause referring to
past time (provided that such a clause has the verb at its

---

[1] i.e. the distant past, or the past continuing into the present. It is
however rarely used after a Future Perfect or after a Prophetic Perfect.

head, and is connected with a previous clause by the conjunction 'and'), even though the action of the second clause does not follow upon one expressed by the first: e.g.

$$\text{אִשָּׁה אַלְמָנָה אָנִי וַיָּמָת אִישִׁי}$$

I am a widow, and my husband died (2 Sam. xiv. 5)

N.B. In sentences of this kind, which are not very common[1], the Imperfect with Wāw Consecutive is used somewhat loosely, to denote an idea which is parallel, not subsequent, to that of the preceding clause, but which is naturally placed second in a narrative. It must not however be supposed that the Imperfect with Wāw Consecutive can ever express a real Pluperfect[2]. When it is necessary to interrupt the main narrative by some explanatory clause, this usually has the subject at its head, so that the close connexion of the verb with the preceding clause is impossible. Such explanatory or, as they are generally called, circumstantial clauses are very common. An example is found in 2 Sam. xviii. 18, viz.

וְאַבְשָׁלוֹם לָקַח וַיַּצֶּב־לוֹ *Now Absalom had taken and set up for himself etc.* In this instance the Hebrew merely states that Absalom did take etc., and from the absence of the consecutive tense makes it clear that the taking

---

[1] The more usual form of the sentence quoted above would be as follows: אִשָּׁה אַלְמָנָה אָנִי וְאִישִׁי מֵת.

[2] The passages where this is apparently the case may be explained either by the fact that large portions of the Old Testament are a compilation of documents originally quite distinct, as for example Gen. xii. 1 (see A. V.), or by confusions in the text as in Isaiah xxxviii. 21, 22.

was not subsequent to the events just recorded[1].   On the
other hand וַיִּקַּח אַבְשָׁלוֹם would mean *And Absalom took*
etc. after the events just recorded.

III.   We have seen that the Imperfect with Wāw
Consecutive denotes the development of an action in
close connexion with a preceding clause.   It is not therefore surprising that we should find it even after a clause
which does not contain a verb, as, for example, a mark of
time : e.g.

וּכְעֵת מוּתָהּ וַתְּדַבֵּרְנָה

And at the time of her death they spoke (1 Sam. iv. 20)

בִּשְׁנַת מוֹת הַמֶּלֶךְ עֻזִּיָּהוּ וָאֶרְאֶה

In the year that King Uzziah died I saw (Isaiah vi. 1)

N.B.   Constructions of this kind may be explained
thus.   The Hebrew as a rule shuns long sentences,
preferring to present to the hearer one by one ideas
which in English are naturally combined into one
sentence.   Thus in the example just given the words
בִּשְׁנַת מוֹת הַמֶּלֶךְ suggest one idea, viz. that of the time,
while the following Imperfect with Wāw Consecutive
suggests another idea, viz. that of an action connected
with the former idea and indeed developed out of it.   It
is impossible, as has been already pointed out, to translate
Hebrew into English without employing limitations
foreign to the former language; but we may perhaps
paraphrase the above sentence thus: "Think of an

---

[1] See on the Perfect, § V, note.   It cannot be too strongly insisted
upon that the Hebrew did not think of an action as a Pluperfect.

occasion in the year of King Uzziah's death, and then imagine me beginning to see."

IV. Similarly the Imperfect with Wāw Consecutive may stand after a *casus pendens*: e.g.

וַיְהִי כָּל־יוֹדְעוֹ מֵאִתְּמוֹל שִׁלְשֹׁם וַיִּרְאוּ וְהִנֵּה וגו'

*And it came to pass, that all whosoever had known him
previously saw, and behold, etc.* (1 Sam. x. 11)

וַיְהִי כָּל־הַבָּא אֶל־הַמָּקוֹם אֲשֶׁר נָפַל שָׁם עֲשָׂהאֵל
וַיָּמֹת וַיַּעֲמֹדוּ

*And it came to pass, that all, whosoever came to the
place where Asahel fell down and died, stood still*
(2 Sam. ii. 23)

N.B. In the two last instances the Imperfects with Wāw Consecutive, וַיִּרְאוּ and וַיַּעֲמֹדוּ, follow upon the *casus pendentes*. The וַיְהִי at the beginning of these sentences is merely used to connect them with what precedes. This indeed is true of all those sentences beginning with וַיְהִי, in which an adverbial clause intervenes between the וַיְהִי and the following Imperfect with Wāw Consecutive. וַיְהִי **is never followed immediately by another Imperfect with Wāw Consecutive,** though it may be followed by a clause in which the nominative stands first, as is the case when it is desired to link with a preceding clause either some description introductory to the subsequent narrative, as in Gen. xi. 1, 1 Sam. i. 2, or two simultaneous actions (according to the idiom described below in Exceptions to the Rule of Wāw Consecutive, § III.), as in 2 Kings ii. 11, 2 Kings xx. 4. With the exception of some passages in which וַיְהִי is obviously followed by its nominative[1], it would perhaps be correct to say that in all cases וַיְהִי is a mere link to the preceding sentence, and all that follows it is in apposition to it.

V. Hitherto we have described the Imperfect with Wāw Consecutive as the sequence of a completed act or state. There are some passages in which it appears to follow a present, or even a future. A careful examination of such passages, however, will shew that the original meaning is never lost. Thus for example we find,

$$\text{יהוה......מוֹרִיד שְׁאוֹל וַיָּעַל}$$

Jehovah bringeth down to Sheôl and then bringeth up
(1 Sam. ii. 6)

$$\text{חֹנֶה מַלְאַךְ יהוה סָבִיב לִירֵאָיו וַיְחַלְּצֵם}$$

The Angel of Jehovah encampeth round about those that fear Him, and delivereth them (Psalm xxxiv. 8)

---

[1] As is the case in וַיְהִי אוֹר (Gen. i. 3). It is however difficult to resist the conviction that the Masoretes have sometimes joined with וַיְהִי a word which really stands at the head of a sentence that contains no verb. Thus, for example, in Gen. xxv. 20, although יִצְחָק is connected by the accents with וַיְהִי, the sentence should probably be translated, '*And it came to pass*, Isaac was 40 years old when he married, etc.,' not '*And Isaac became* 40 years old, etc.' Compare Gen. xi. 1 where the following nominative is feminine, and 1 Sam. i. 2 where it is plural.

N.B. It must be borne in mind that in such sentences the Participle is not a real present. The poet does not mean to state that at the moment at which he is speaking Jehovah is bringing down to Sheôl, nor yet that the Angel of Jehovah is actually encamping. Just as the Participle may be used with the definite Article simply to qualify a noun without any thought of the *time* of the action denoted by it (e.g. הַיֹּצֵא Joshua v. 4), so here the Participles state predicatively distinguishing acts of Jehovah or His Angel, of which the time is not specified, but which assuredly go on to completion. There is therefore nothing anomalous in the fact that the sequence of such acts is represented by the Imperfect · with Wāw Consecutive. In the first illustration given above it must not be supposed that the two clauses יְהֹוָה מֵמִית and מוֹרִיד שְׁאוֹל וַיָּעַל and וּמְחַיֶּה are *synonymous* parallels. The two Participles מֵמִית וּמְחַיֶּה merely state coordinately the fact that Jehovah is One to Whom may be assigned the actions both of putting to death and also of preserving alive. On the other hand the second clause מוֹרִיד שְׁאוֹל וַיָּעַל states that *after* bringing down to Sheôl Jehovah goes on to bring up again. Similarly in the second illustration, if the first verb should not be pointed חֹנֶה as the Perfect, the sense is that the Angel is one who encamps and the effect of this encampment when completed is the deliverance of those who fear Jehovah[1].

---

[1] Such instances of the Imperfect with Wāw Consecutive after a Participle as הַמֶּלֶךְ בֹּכֶה וַיִּתְאַבֵּל (2 Sam. xix. 2) may be explained on the analogy of 2 Sam. xiv. 5, quoted above, § II. Translate *The king is weeping, and has put on mourning* (lit. *has made himself a mourner*), cf. Jeremiah vi. 13, 14.

VI. The Imperfect with Wāw Consecutive is occasionally found in sentences which English idiom puts
into a conditional form, in which case it represents the
effect of a certain condition. There is not however in the
Hebrew any division of the sentence into *protasis* and
apodosis. The Perfect in the first clause is used according to the usages described above (see on the Perfect,
§§ VI., IX. and X.), and the Imperfect with Wāw Consecutive merely expresses its consequence. Examples are,

$$\text{נָשַׁף בָּהֶם וַיִּבָשׁוּ}$$

When he has blown upon them, they wither (Isaiah xl. 24)

$$\text{בָּא זָדוֹן וַיָּבֹא קָלוֹן}$$

When pride has come, humiliation comes (Prov. xi. 2)

$$\text{כִּי חַרְבְּךָ הֵנַפְתָּ עָלֶיהָ וַתְּחַלְלֶהָ}$$

*For when thou hast wielded thy hatchet on it, thou hast
profaned it* (Exodus xx. 25)

$$\text{לוּא הִקְשַׁבְתָּ לְמִצְוֹתָי וַיְהִי כַנָּהָר שְׁלוֹמֶךָ}$$

*If only thou hadst hearkened to my commandments, thy
prosperity had been like a river* (Isaiah xlviii. 18)

[In this case וַיְהִי is not the *apodosis*, but the completion of the first condition specified in the *protasis*.
The real *apodosis* of the sentence is suppressed, but it
may be supplied somewhat as follows: "If thou hadst
hearkened to my commandments and as a consequence
thy prosperity had been like a river etc., then it would
have been well."]

VII. Similarly the Imperfect with Wāw Consecutive may be used to express the result of an interrogative clause, such result being introduced in English by ' so that ': e.g.

לָמָה אָמַרְתָּ אֲחֹתִי הִוא וָאֶקַּח אֹתָהּ

Why didst thou say to me, She is my sister, so that I took her ? (Gen. xii. 19)

לָמָה שַׂמְתַּנִי לְמִפְגָּע לָךְ וָאֶהְיֶה וגו׳

Why hast Thou made me Thy target, so that I have become, etc. ? (Job vii. 20)

[In these examples the לָמָה asks the reason of the series of actions, expressed by the Perfect and the following Imperfect with Wāw Consecutive. Thus we may paraphrase the passage from Gen. xii. 19 as follows: " Why was it the case that thou saidst to me, She is my sister, and I consequently took her ? "]

VIII. Occasionally the Imperfect with Wāw Consecutive is found in passages which cannot well be classed under any of the above heads, where, however, the meaning is clear. It must be remembered that, although the Imperfect with Wāw Consecutive originally merely denoted an action *as following upon another completed action*, it has from its frequent use in narrative come itself to denote *the completion of each successive act*. Accordingly we sometimes find it used, especially in passages of a later date, to express the *completion* of an act following upon an *incomplete* act. Thus, for example, we find

K. 4

כִּי עַתָּה תָּבוֹא אֵלֶיךָ וַתֵּלֶא תִּגַּע עָדֶיךָ וַתִּבָּהֵל

For now it cometh[1] unto thee, and thou art overcome;
it reacheth unto thee and thou art panic-stricken

(Job iv. 5)

[The sentence means that, while the coming is not
yet complete, Job's panic is complete. This construction
is not however common. The ordinary prose idiom would
be as follows: תָּבוֹא אֵלֶיךָ וְהִנֵּה נִלְאֵיתָ]

IX. One other illustration will suffice to shew the
sense acquired by the Imperfect with Wāw Consecutive.
In Ps. cxliv. 3 there is an echo of Ps. viii. 5, in a somewhat
altered form, viz.

מָה אָדָם וַתֵּדָעֵהוּ בֶּן־אֱנוֹשׁ וַתְּחַשְּׁבֵהוּ

What is man, that Thou shouldest have known him, or the
son of mortal man, that Thou shouldest have taken account
of him?

[In the above sentence the force of the Imperfect with
Wāw Consecutive may be seen by substituting some
definite predicate for the interrogative מָה: e.g. *Man is*
(great), and so Thou hast known him, and the son of mortal
man is honourable, and so Thou hast taken account of him.

It must not however be supposed that the וַתֵּדָעֵהוּ and
וַתְּחַשְּׁבֵהוּ of this verse are exactly synonymous with the

---

[1] For this use of the Imperfect see above on the Imperfect, § I, b.

כִּי תְזְכְּרֶנּוּ and כִּי תִפְקְדֶנּוּ of Ps. viii. 5[1]. The latter phrases denote *habitual* acts: by the former the psalmist means to express the completion of the acts יְדַע and חִשֵׁב. The ordinary way of expressing this however would be by כִּי followed by the Perfect.]

---

[1] It is not altogether unnecessary to protest against the assumption that parallel passages which convey the same general sense are of necessity exactly synonymous. The general sense expressed by συνε-σταυρώθη (Rom. vi. 6) is, with the difference of the person, the same as that expressed by συνεσταύρωμαι (Gal. ii. 20), but no one supposes that an Aorist is synonymous with a Perfect. May we not plead that the same precision which is employed in translating the text of the Greek Testament should be likewise employed in translating the Hebrew Bible?

THE PERFECT WITH WĀW CONSECUTIVE.

We have seen that, although past actions are usually conceived as complete, and future actions as incomplete, it may nevertheless be desirable for the sake of greater vividness or emphasis to paint each detail of the former, or to represent the completion of the latter. We have an instance of the former idiom in Isaiah vi. 4, where the Imperfect יִמָּלֵא brings vividly before our mind the whole process of the filling of the temple, and of the latter idiom in בִּלַּע הַמָּוֶת לָנֶצַח (Isaiah xxv. 8), where the representation of the annihilation of death as accomplished implies in the most emphatic manner the certainty of this annihilation.

We have seen that in describing a series of past actions the Hebrew represents each successive action as developed out of the one before it, the attention of the hearer having been directed to the past by a Perfect or by some mark of time.

It now remains for us to consider the method employed by the Hebrew in representing a series of actions in the future. We will take as an example the sentence, *He will put forth his hand and will take, etc.* The first verb of this sentence, being a simple Future (whereof the action is conceived as incomplete), will naturally be expressed in Hebrew by the Imperfect יִשְׁלַח. The second verb, however, is also a simple Future, and we might therefore expect that it would be expressed likewise by the Imperfect יִקַּח. But in a sentence consisting of two similar tenses coupled together by *and* וְ, there would be nothing to denote that the second action was conceived as the consequence of the first. The two actions might in fact be parallel or simultaneous[1]. But in the case of two successive future actions however uncertain the first may be, the latter is, generally speaking, *certain relatively to the first.* Thus in the sentence which we have taken for an illustration, though the putting forth of the hand may be uncertain, yet, assuming that the hand will be put forth, the taking of the fruit may be regarded as a certain consequence. But we have seen that, when it is desired to express the certainty of a future action, the Perfect is used : accordingly in the instance before us *he will take* will naturally be expressed by the Perfect לָקַח, and the fact that this Perfect of Certainty is immediately connected with the preceding clause by the conjunction וְ *and* implies that the action of taking is regarded as certain in relation to the action of putting forth the hand. The sentence will therefore run יִשְׁלַח יָדוֹ וְלָקַח.

N.B. It will be observed that in this construction the conjunction has its ordinary form. It is however by no means certain that originally Wāw Consecutive assumed different forms with the Perfect and with the Imperfect. We have seen that the original form of the conjunction

---

[1] As for example in the sentence אָז יְדַלֵּג כְּאַיָּל פִּסֵּחַ וְתָרֹן לְשׁוֹן אִלֵּם *Then shall the lame man leap as a hart, and the tongue of the dumb shall shout for joy* (Isaiah xxxv. 6).

was *wa*, the doubling of the preformative letter of the
Imperfect being probably merely euphonic and analogous
to the doubling of the מ in לָמָּה. Although it is obvious
that there must always have been some means of distinguishing between the Imperfect with Wāw Consecutive
and with the ordinary weak wāw, it is nevertheless open
to question whether such a doubling existed in primitive
Hebrew: it may possibly have arisen unconsciously from
an effort to keep the syllable *wa* clear and distinct. In
the case of the Perfect, on the other hand, though it is
probable that the conjunction was originally pronounced
with the same vowel, the first consonant was not doubled
and the *wa* was therefore reduced to וְ. It is somewhat
difficult to find a reason for this anomaly. It may be
that, since all Imperfects (from whatever root they may
be derived, or to whatever conjugation they may belong)
begin in the several persons with the same consonants,
the emphatic form of Wāw with the Imperfect tended to
crystallise into וַ, whereas before the various consonants
with which the Perfect may begin, such crystallisation
was less likely to take place, and the conjunction being
usually two places from the tone was accordingly pointed
in the ordinary way[1].

One other peculiarity of this Perfect of Certainty with

---

[1] In the eight words quoted above from Gen. viii. 22 וְקָצִיר is not less
closely connected with זֶרַע than וָחֹם with וְקֹר, the *sh'wā* in the former
word being due merely to the distance from the tone. But in the *spoken*
language the difference in the pronunciation of the syllable *wa*, if it
existed at all, must have been very slight.

Occasionally before a monosyllabic Perfect the Wāw Consecutive is
pointed וָ, as for example in וָחַי (Gen. iii. 22), but this pointing is not
uniform.

Wāw or, as it is usually called, the Perfect with Wāw Consecutive, is the shifting of the tone. Whereas Wāw Consecutive with the Imperfect tends to draw the tone back to the penultimate, with the Perfect, on the other hand, it tends to throw it forward from the penultimate to the final syllable, e.g. וְשָׁמַתִּי, וְלָקַחְתָּ. But it is doubtful whether this shifting of the tone is primitive, for just as we can only explain the first Ḳāmeṣ in the word לָקְחָה by postulating an earlier form לָקָחָה (a supposition which is confirmed by the pausal form לָקָחָה), so the pointing וְלָקַחְתָּ can only be explained on the supposition that, when the short vowel of the first syllable of the Perfect was heightened into Ḳāmeṣ, the accent was on the second syllable, to which indeed it returns in pause.

We have seen that there is a close affinity between the so-called Perfect of Certainty and this Perfect with Wāw Consecutive. As in the case of the Imperfect with Wāw Consecutive, so in this idiom also the Perfect must stand at the head of its clause, for if the emphasis[1] be on any other word, even the negative, the intimate connexion of the act represented as complete with that represented as incomplete is overlooked[2].

I. In representing a series of future actions, therefore, the Hebrew, after directing his hearer's attention to the

---

[1] The first word of a sentence is always the most emphatic.

[2] It is most important to bear in mind that both in the case of the Perfect and of the Imperfect with Wāw Consecutive there is *no change whatever in the essential meaning of the tense*. The emphatic Wāw is merely a strong conjunction shewing that the subsequent action is most intimately connected with the preceding.

future by the use of the Imperfect, expresses each
successive action by the Perfect with Wāw Consecutive : e.g.

אֵלַי יֵצֵא יָצוֹא וְעָמַד וְקָרָא

To me he will come out¹, and will stand and call
(2 Kings v. 11)

אֵצֵא וְהָיִיתִי רוּחַ שֶׁקֶר

I will go forth, and become a spirit of lying
(1 Kings xxii. 22)

II.   It is not however necessary that Wāw Consecutive
with the Perfect should actually be preceded by an
Imperfect.   It may be used where there is an idea of
an incomplete or future action, even though that idea
is not expressed by an Imperfect.   Thus it is found,

(*a*)   after a Participle : e.g.

הִנֵּה יהוה רֹכֵב עַל־עָב קַל וּבָא מִצְרַיִם

Lo, Jehovah rideth on a swift cloud, and will come to Egypt
(Isaiah xix. 1)

הִנְנִי מַמְטִיר לָכֶם לֶחֶם מִן־הַשָּׁמַיִם וְיָצָא הָעָם וְלָקְטוּ

*Lo, I will rain food for you from the heavens; and the
people shall go forth and gather* (Ex. xvi. 4)

---

¹ The emphatic position of אֵלַי ' to *me* ' shews Naaman's sense of his
own importance.   In consequence of this, however, the verb loses somewhat of its emphasis.   But as Naaman wishes to put emphasis on the
verb also (contrasting his own expectation that the prophet would come
out with the actual fact of his staying indoors), the lost emphasis is
more than restored by the use of the Infinitive Absolute.

(*b*) after a mark of time : e.g.

עֶרֶב וִידַעְתֶּם

At even ye shall know (Ex. xvi. 6)

בְּיוֹם אֲכָלְכֶם מִמֶּנּוּ וְנִפְקְחוּ עֵינֵיכֶם

In the day of your eating of it your eyes will be opened
(Gen. iii. 5)

(*c*) after a Prophetic Perfect : e.g.

לָכֵן הִרְחִיבָה שְׁאוֹל נַפְשָׁה וּפָעֲרָה פִּיהָ

Therefore shall the appetite of Sheôl be increased (lit. *shall
Sheôl increase her appetite*), *and she shall open wide her
mouth* (Isaiah v. 14)

לְמַעַנְכֶם ¹שִׁלַּחְתִּי בָבֶלָה וְהוֹרַדְתִּי וגו׳

For your sake I will send to Babylon and bring down, etc.
(Isaiah xliii. 14)

(*d*) after a statement referring to the present or
to the immediate past, the consequence of which is
future : e.g.

נָגַע זֶה עַל־שְׂפָתֶיךָ וְסָר עֲוֹנֶךָ

This has touched thy lips, and so thy guilt shall be removed
(Isaiah vi. 7)

אֵין יִרְאַת אֱלֹהִים בַּמָּקוֹם הַזֶּה וַהֲרָגוּנִי

There is no religion in this place, and so they will kill me
(Gen. xx. 11)

---

¹ In the Masoretic text this word is pointed as a Piel, but the Ḳal is
more natural in the sense which the word evidently has here.

(e)   after a *casus pendens:* e.g.

הַמְדַבֵּר אֵלֶיךָ וַהֲבֵאתוֹ[1] אֵלַי

Whosoever speaketh unto thee, thou shalt bring him to me
(2 Sam. xiv. 10)

כִּי כָל־סְאוֹן סֹאֵן בְּרַעַשׁ וְשִׂמְלָה מְגוֹלָלָה[2] בְדָמִים
וְהָיְתָה לִשְׂרֵפָה

For every boot of noisily tramping warrior and garment rolled
(? defiled) in blood shall become a bonfire (Isaiah ix. 4)

III.   Similarly when a series of actions is desired,
each successive action after the first is expressed by the
Perfect with Wāw Consecutive.

Thus we find it,

(a)   after an Imperfect expressing a command : e.g.

מִזְבַּח אֲדָמָה תַּעֲשֶׂה־לִּי וְזָבַחְתָּ עָלָיו

An altar of earth shalt thou make unto me, and thou shalt
sacrifice thereon (Ex. xx. 24)

וְלֹא תִשָּׁבְעוּ בִשְׁמִי לַשָּׁקֶר וְחִלַּלְתָּ אֶת־שֵׁם אֱלֹהֶיךָ

Neither shalt thou swear falsely by My name, and so
profane the name of thy God (Lev. xix. 12)

(b)   after a Jussive : e.g.

יְהִי מְאֹרֹת......וְהָיוּ לְאֹתֹת

Let there be lights......and let them be signs (Gen. i. 14)

מְנֹאָלָה ? [2]   כְּצ״ל [1]

אֵל שַׁדַּי יִתֵּן לָכֶם רַחֲמִים לִפְנֵי הָאִישׁ וְשִׁלַּח
לָכֶם אֶת־אֲחִיכֶם

*May El Shaddai give you favour before the man, and may
he set free your brother* (Gen. xliii. 14).

(c)   after a Cohortative: e.g.

נִכְרְתָה בְּרִית......וְהָיָה לְעֵד

Let us make a covenant......and let it be a witness
(Gen. xxxi. 44)

נִקְרְבָה בְּאַחַד הַמְּקֹמוֹת וְלַנּוּ וגו׳

*Let us draw near to some place or other, and let us spend
the night, etc.* (Judges xix. 13)

(d)   after an Imperative: e.g.

כָּל־הַחַיָּה......¹הוֹצֵא אִתָּךְ וְשָׁרְצוּ

All the living things......take out with thee, and let them swarm
(Gen. viii. 17)

צֵא וְעָמַדְתָּ בָהָר לִפְנֵי יהוה

Go forth, and stand upon the mountain before Jehovah
(1 Kings xix. 11)

(e)   after an Infinitive Absolute with the sense of
an Imperative: e.g.

הָלוֹךְ וְרָחַצְתָּ שֶׁבַע־פְּעָמִים בַּיַּרְדֵּן

Go and wash seven times in the Jordan (2 Kings v. 10)

---

¹ כצ״ל

הָלוֹךְ אֶל־בֵּית הָרֵכָבִים וְדִבַּרְתָּ אוֹתָם

Go to the house of the Rechabites, and speak with them
(Jeremiah xxxv. 2)

N.B. Although it is frequently impossible in an
English translation to distinguish between a Perfect
with Wāw Consecutive and a Cohortative, Jussive, or
Imperative with simple *wāw*, when a Cohortative, Jussive,
or Imperative has preceded, there is nevertheless a shade
of difference in the Hebrew which must not be ignored.
We have seen that, when two parallel clauses, each
expressing a desire, are coupled together by simple *wāw*,
it is *the end chiefly desired* which is expressed by the
latter verb, and a final particle may therefore be used in
translating it : e.g. שִׁמְעוּ וּתְחִי נַפְשְׁכֶם *Hear,* that *your
soul* may *live* (Isaiah lv. 3). On the other hand the
construction of the Perfect with Wāw Consecutive represents each of the successive actions as *willed in turn* by
the speaker, and expresses a series of directions or a
series of actions each of which is more or less desired.
שִׁמְעוּ וְחָיְתָה נַפְשְׁכֶם would mean, to adopt a paraphrase,
'I desire that *first* you should hear and *afterwards* your
soul should live.' These two constructions are both found
in 2 Kings v. 10, quoted above, and the sentence is a
good illustration of the difference in their meanings. The
passage runs, הָלוֹךְ וְרָחַצְתָּ שֶׁבַע־פְּעָמִים בַּיַּרְדֵּן וְיָשֹׁב
בְּשָׂרְךָ לְךָ וּטְהָר which may be translated, *Go and wash*
(a series of directions) *seven times in the Jordan,* that *thy
flesh* may *be restored, and thou* mayest *be clean* (the end
chiefly desired).

The Perfect with Wāw Consecutive never expresses

the purpose of the preceding action.   Thus, for example,
in 1 Kings xvii. 12 the verbs ...... וּבָאתִי וַעֲשִׂיתִיהוּ

וַאֲכַלְנֻהוּ וָמָתְנוּ merely express the series of actions which
the widow has resolved upon and the subsequent starvation
which she considers inevitable.   The " that I may go "
and " that we may eat " of the English version are quite
wrong.

IV.   The Perfect with Wāw Consecutive is likewise
used after an Imperfect when the latter possesses a
frequentative sense, not only

(a)   in the future : e.g.

יָבוֹא כָל־בָּשָׂר לְהִשְׁתַּחֲוֹת לְפָנַי ...... וְיָצְאוּ

All flesh shall come (month by month and week by week) *to
worship before me......and they shall go forth*
(Isaiah lxvi. 23, 24)

נָכוֹן יִהְיֶה הַר בֵּית יהוה...... וְנָהֲרוּ אֵלָיו כָּל־הַגּוֹיִם

*The mountain of Jehovah's house shall be established......and
all the nations shall flow unto it* (Isaiah ii. 2)

and

(b)   in the present : e.g.

עַל־כֵּן יַעֲזָב־אִישׁ אֶת־אָבִיו וְאֶת־אִמּוֹ וְדָבַק בְּאִשְׁתּוֹ

*Therefore a man leaves his father and his mother and cleaves
to his wife* (Gen. ii. 24)

כַּאֲשֶׁר יִמָּצֵא הַתִּירוֹשׁ בָּאֶשְׁכּוֹל וְאָמַר אַל־תַּשְׁחִיתֵהוּ

*As the sweet juice is found in the cluster, and one says,
Destroy it not* (Isaiah lxv. 8)

but also

(c)   in the past: e.g.

וְאֵד יַעֲלֶה מִן־הָאָרֶץ וְהִשְׁקָה אֶת־כָּל־פְּנֵי הָאֲדָמָה

And a mist used to go up from the earth, and water all the surface of the ground (Gen. ii. 6)

וּמֹשֶׁה יִקַּח אֶת־הָאֹהֶל וְנָטָה וגו׳

Now Moses used to take the tent, and pitch it, etc.
(Ex. xxxiii. 7)

[The use of the Perfect with Wāw Consecutive in such cases, which is extremely common, seems somewhat inconsistent with the explanation given above which connects the Perfect with Wāw Consecutive with the Perfect of Certainty. Logically there seems to be no reason why the Imperfect with Wāw Consecutive should not have been used in such cases. The probable explanation is that, as the Imperfect with Wāw Consecutive became stereotyped as the sequence of a Perfect or Perfect idea, so the Perfect with Wāw Consecutive became stereotyped as the sequence of an Imperfect; and since in all cases where the Imperfect refers to the present or the future the Perfect with Wāw Consecutive is the natural sequence, it has come to be used in the past also.]

N.B.   For the use of the Perfect with Wāw Consecutive after an Infinitive Absolute see below.

V.   The Perfect with Wāw Consecutive is likewise used in the *apodosis* of conditional sentences: e.g.

אִם־יֵשׁ אָחִינוּ הַקָּטֹן אִתָּנוּ וְיָרַדְנוּ

If our youngest brother be with us, we will go down
(Gen. xliv. 26)

אִם־תֵּלְכִי עִמִּי וְהָלַכְתִּי

If thou wilt go with me, I will go (Judges iv. 8)

אִם־כֹּה יֹאמַר נְקֻדִּים יִהְיֶה שְׂכָרֶךָ וְיָלְדוּ כָל־הַצֹּאן נְקֻדִּים

If he said (whenever he said) *thus, The spotted shall be thy
wages, then all the sheep would bear spotted* (Gen. xxxi. 8)

וְאִם־יָשַׁבְנוּ פֹה וָמָתְנוּ

And if we tarry (shall have tarried) *here, we shall die*
(2 Kings vii. 4)

[1]אִם־שָׁכַבְתִּי וְאָמַרְתִּי מָתַי אָקוּם

As soon as I have lain down, I say When shall I arise?
(Job vii. 4)

N.B. The use of *wāw* in the *apodosis* of a conditional
sentence is strange to our way of thinking, but it is not
confined to the case of Wāw Consecutive with the Perfect.
Thus we find אִם הַשְּׂמֹאל וְאֵימִנָה וְאִם־הַיָּמִין וְאַשְׂמְאִילָה
If (thou goest) *to the left hand, I will go to the right; and
if* (thou goest) *to the right hand, I will go to the left*
(Gen. xiii. 9). The explanation seems to be that אִם
does not *subordinate* a clause in Hebrew in the way that
if subordinates one in English. Compare the use of
אִם......הֲ to express *utrum......an*. Wāw is also found
after other particles such as כִּי, e.g. Deut. xxi. 18, 19.

---

[1] אִם is commonly used as a temporal particle before a Perfect when
the time of the action is indefinite, cf. Ps. lxxviii. 34 אִם־הֲרָגָם וּדְרָשׁוּהוּ
Whenever He had slain them, they would seek Him.

VI. The Perfect with Wāw Consecutive is also found in many sentences which must be put into a hypothetical form in English, but which are not strictly hypothetical in Hebrew : e.g.

וּדְפָקוּם יוֹם אֶחָד וָמֵתוּ כָּל־הַצֹּאן

And if they overdrive them one day, all the sheep will die
(Gen. xxxiii. 13)

וּקְרָאָהוּ אָסוֹן בַּדֶּרֶךְ אֲשֶׁר תֵּלְכוּ־בָהּ וְהוֹרַדְתֶּם
אֶת־שֵׂיבָתִי בְּיָגוֹן שְׁאוֹלָה

And if harm befall him on the journey on which ye go, ye will bring down my gray hairs in sorrow to Sheôl
(Gen. xlii. 38)

[In the above sentences what is possible or probable is stated as certain together with its result.]

VII. Sometimes in sentences similar to those described in the foregoing section it may be necessary to translate the Perfect with Wāw Consecutive as an interrogative. Such sentences however are not, strictly speaking, interrogative. They are rather statements which are sarcastically[1] assumed to be the thought of the persons addressed: e.g.

---

[1] It may be laid down as a definite rule that whenever the interrogative ה is omitted in a sentence which is apparently interrogative there is always a touch of irony. A good illustration of this idiom is found in Isaiah i. 18, viz. לְכוּ־נָא וְנִוָּכְחָה יֹאמַר יהוה אִם־יִהְיוּ חֲטָאֵיכֶם כַשָּׁנִים כַּשֶּׁלֶג יַלְבִּינוּ *Come and let us argue, Jehovah keeps saying ; if your sins be as crimson, are they to be white as snow?* The word וְנִוָּכְחָה *let us argue* shews that the sentence is virtually interrogative, for there is no argument in the promise which the English version understands here,

בְּנֶשֶׁךְ נָתַן וְתַרְבִּית לָקַח וָחָי

If he has given forth upon usury and has taken increase,
shall he live? (Ezek. xviii. 13)

[We may paraphrase the above sentence thus: " A
man may have given forth upon usury and taken increase,
and yet, according to your notions of fairness, he is to
live !"]

רַבּוּ עֲבָדִים הַמִּתְפָּרְצִים אִישׁ מִפְּנֵי אֲדֹנָיו וְלָקַחְתִּי
אֶת־לַחְמִי וגו׳

There are many servants now-a-days that break away from
their several masters, and so I forsooth am to take my
bread, etc.! (1 Sam. xxv. 10, 11)

N.B. Similar sentences are found where owing to
the presence of the negative the Imperfect is used instead
of the Perfect with Wāw Consecutive: e.g. הֵן נִזְבַּח
אֶת־תּוֹעֲבַת מִצְרַיִם לְעֵינֵיהֶם וְלֹא יִסְקְלֻנוּ *Lo! we are to*
sacrifice that which is an abomination to the Egyptians
before their eyes, and they will not stone us! (Ex. viii. 22.)

---

and which moreover is unsuitable to the context. We may paraphrase
the sentence thus: " You seem to imagine that, even when your sins are
as glaring as crimson, you have but to come to the sanctuary and hold a
sacrificial feast, and they will be as white as snow !"

ADDITIONAL NOTE ON THE PERFECT
WITH WĀW CONSECUTIVE.

There are some instances in which the Perfect with Wāw Consecutive appears after an Infinitive Absolute to express an action simultaneous with that of the Infinitive : e.g. הֹלְכִים הָלוֹךְ וְתָקְעוּ *going on and trumpeting as they went* (Joshua vi. 13), וַתֵּלֶךְ הָלוֹךְ וְזָעֲקָה *and she went away, crying aloud as she went* (2 Sam. xiii. 19). This construction however is not very certain, for, although there is nothing intrinsically improbable in this use of the Perfect with Wāw Consecutive, further proof of it is desiderated. It is noteworthy that according to the Masoretic text there are four variations of the common idiom by which two or more Infinitives Absolute coupled by *wāw* express simultaneous actions qualifying the main action of the sentence. Thus we have

(1) the Infinitive Absolute followed by the Perfect with Wāw Consecutive, as in Joshua vi. 13, 2 Sam. xiii. 19, quoted above,

(2) the Infinitive Absolute followed by the Imperfect with Wāw Consecutive, as in 1 Sam. xix. 23, 2 Sam. xvi. 13,

(3) the Infinitive Absolute followed by the Participle, as in Gen. xxvi. 13, 2 Sam. xvi. 5, Jerem. xli. 6,

(4) the Infinitive Absolute followed by an Adjective, as in Judges iv. 24, 1 Sam. xiv. 19, 2 Sam. v. 10, 1 Chron. xi. 9.

It must however be confessed that in the existing condition of the Masoretic text it is difficult to feel convinced that all these variations actually existed, since in some instances it is possible to restore the ordinary idiom by merely altering the points, and in others there is some doubt as to the correctness of the consonantal text. Thus in examining the passages referred to above we find that doubt is thrown on וְתִקְעוּ (Joshua vi. 13) by the occurrence of the normal וְתִקְעוּ in *v.* 9, while the *K'thîbh* in the latter part of the verse implies the work of a 'sleepy scribe.' Again in וַיְקַלֵּל (2 Sam. xvi. 13) it is remarkable that we have a variation from the וּמְקַלֵּל in *v.* 5 of the same chapter, and moreover the presence of וְעִפָּר (Perf. with Wāw Consec.) in the same verse seems to imply some confusion in the text. Again וְגָדֵל (Gen. xxvi. 13) might be pointed וִגְדֹל (compare 2 Sam. v. 10), וְרֹב (1 Sam. xiv. 19) וְרָב, וְקָשֹׁה (Judges iv. 24) וְקָשָׁה (compare קֹב Num. xxiii. 25, שֹׁל Ruth ii. 16), whereas וְגָדוֹל (2 Sam. v. 10, 1 Chron. xi. 9) has the proper form of the Infinitive Absolute.

It will thus be seen that variation 1 rests on the solitary evidence of וְזַעֲקָה (2 Sam. xiii. 19), unless וְגָעוּ (1 Sam. vi. 12) was intended by the author to be read וְגָעוּ; variation 2 depends on וַיִּתְנַבֵּא (1 Sam. xix. 23); variation 3 on וּמְקַלֵּל (2 Sam. xvi. 5), whereas variation 4 has no certain proof. In 1 Sam. xix. 23 it would be possible to connect the הָלוֹךְ with the preceding verb on the analogy of 2 Sam. iii. 24 (where however see LXX), translating 'and he went right on, and he prophesied.' This division is actually implied by the accents in Joshua vi. 13, but the analogy of other passages is against it.

On the other hand in 2 Sam. xii. 16 the accentuation of
צוֹם, which connects it with וַיָּצָם and separates it from the
following וּבָא, is probably correct. The Infinitive Absolute in this verse is to be understood on the analogy of
שָׁפוֹט (Gen. xix. 9), i.e. as giving emphasis to the preceding
finite verb. Translate, '*And David sought God on the
child's behalf, and David actually fasted* (an extraordinary
act seeing that the child was still alive), *and he would go
in and pass the night lying on the ground.*'

In view of the circumstances considered above, although
we are scarcely justified in arbitrarily altering the text,
we may refuse to admit the above variations among the
recognised rules of Hebrew Syntax unless further proof
be forthcoming.

It is hardly necessary to say that those cases in which
the Participle of הלך is followed by another Participle
or by an adjective, which is virtually equivalent to the
Participle of a stative verb, as in Ex. xix. 19, 1 Sam. ii. 26,
2 Sam. xv. 12, Jonah i. 11, 13 etc., present no difficulty
and require no comment.

EXCEPTIONS TO THE RULE OF
WĀW CONSECUTIVE.

It is evident from the foregoing pages that the Perfect with Wāw Consecutive may be used in every place where the simple Imperfect might have stood if the conjunction 'and' had been absent; and that, conversely, the Imperfect with Wāw Consecutive takes under similar circumstances the place of a simple Perfect. It must be borne in mind, that, with the exceptions given below, whenever it is necessary to connect two clauses by means of the conjunction 'and,' the verb in the second clause must have Wāw Consecutive.

I. Wāw Consecutive is not used when the second clause is only explanatory of, or synonymous with, the first clause : e.g.

וַאֲנִי זָקַנְתִּי וָשַׂבְתִּי

And I am old and gray-headed (1 Sam. xii. 2)

בָּנִים גִּדַּלְתִּי וְרוֹמַמְתִּי

Children have I reared and brought up (Isaiah i. 2)

אָז יְדַלֵּג כָּאַיָּל פִּסֵּחַ וְתָרֹן לְשׁוֹן אִלֵּם

Then shall the lame man leap as a hart, and the tongue of the dumb shall shout for joy (Isaiah xxxv. 6)

כִּי אִם־תְּכַבְּסִי בַּנֶּתֶר וְתַרְבִּי לָךְ בֹּרִית נִכְתָּם עֲוֹנֵךְ לְפָנַי

For though thou shouldest scour with soda, and take thee
much soap, thy guilt would be indelible before me
(Jerem. ii. 22)

N.B.   This use of weak *wāw*, as it is called, to couple
two similar tenses is not common, and, especially in the
case of the Perfect, it has evidently been avoided even
where it might have been employed.   Thus, for example,
although we cannot say that וּשְׁמַרְתֶּם (Joshua xxii. 3) or
וְשָׁאַלְתָּ (1 Kings iii. 11) violates any of the principles
which have been explained above, since between the
negation of a fact and the affirmation of what is contrasted with it there is no actual sequence, yet the
presence of weak *wāw* in these instances strikes the
reader as unusual.   In fact as a rule the common idiom
either discards *wāw* altogether after a negative sentence,
using instead כִּי or כִּי אִם, or, if it keeps the *wāw*, places
some word other than the verb at the head of the second
clause, or even, though less logically, uses the Imperfect
with Wāw Consecutive as in וַיִּשְׁכָּחֵהוּ (Gen. xl. 23),
וַיֵּשֶׁב (Judges i. 21) etc.

On the other hand there appears to have been less
objection to the use of the Imperfect with weak *wāw*;
perhaps because the Imperfect in most cases exactly
resembles the Jussive and Cohortative, and, as we have
already seen, the Jussive and Cohortative with weak *wāw*
can frequently be used where the Perfect with Wāw
Consecutive might stand, although the two idioms are

not quite synonymous¹. Thus we find וְאָכַתְּב (Deut. x. 2)
where the parallel passage Ex. xxxiv. 1 has וְכָתַבְתִּי,
וְאָשִׁיב (1 Sam. xii. 3), וְנָשִׁיב (1 Kings xii. 9), whereas in
a very similar sentence (Num. xxii. 8) the Perfect with
Wāw Consecutive וַהֲשִׁבֹתִי occurs. It is not however
impossible that such forms are in many cases to be
regarded as Jussives, or, which in the above instances
would be preferable, pointed as Cohortatives².

In the later Hebrew, perhaps under the influence of
Aramaic dialects, the use of Wāw Consecutive was
gradually discontinued: in the earlier books however it
is possible that in several instances where weak *wāw*
appears to be combined with a Perfect, an Infinitive
Absolute was intended by the writer: e.g. וְנָשָׂא (2 Kings
xxiii. 4), וְהִשְׁבִּית (ib. 5), וְנָתַץ (ib. 8), וְטָמֵא (ib. 10).
On the other hand we must remember how easy it would
be for a scribe *accidentally* to leave out a *yôdh* or in the
old character to confuse *hē* and *yôdh*. Moreover in documents of quite early date there are many passages which
are late interpolations. Is it possible to believe that
Genesis xv. 6 was written before the Exile?

---

¹ See above on the Perfect with Wāw Consecutive, § III, note.

² See above, Additional Notes to the Cohortative and Jussive, § III.
The strongest argument against considering such forms as וְאָשִׁיב as
Jussive is the extreme rarity of the Jussive in the first person. On the
other hand the *scriptio plena* of the *ḥireḳ* is not a fatal objection, for in
Aramaic both *wāw* and *yôdh* are used as *matres lectionis* of *short* as well
as long vowels, and there are several instances of similar spelling in the
Hebrew Bible. See, for example, מלוכה (K'thîbh, Judges ix. 8), מלוכי
(ib. 12), probably representing respectively the old pronunciation of the
Imperative m'lŭkha, m'lŭkhî, יְמִישׁוּן (Ps. cxv. 7) from מוּשׁ, זיקות
(Isaiah l. 11) = זִקּוֹת, etc.

II. Wāw Consecutive is not used when some word in
the second clause has to be emphasized in order that it
may be contrasted with something in the first clause.   In
such a case the emphatic word stands first and the verb
not being at the head of the clause is not 'consecutive.'
Thus we find,

וַתֻּקַּח הָאִשָּׁה בֵּית פַּרְעֹה וּלְאַבְרָם הֵיטִיב בַּעֲבוּרָהּ

And the woman was taken into Pharaoh's house, and
Abram he (Pharaoh) *treated kindly on her account*
(Gen. xii. 15, 16)

וַיֵּצֵא אֲלֵהֶם לוֹט הַפֶּתְחָה וְהַדֶּלֶת סָגַר אַחֲרָיו

And Lot went out to the entrance, but the door he
shut after him (Gen. xix. 6)

N.B. In sentences of this sort the *time* can only be
inferred from the context and the action *may* belong to
some earlier occasion, i.e. it may correspond to an English
Pluperfect.   In the latter case however the Nominative is
generally, though not always, placed at the head of the
clause: e.g. וְרָחֵל לָקְחָה אֶת־הַתְּרָפִים *Now it was Rachel*
who had taken the images (Gen. xxxi. 34).   On the other
hand we find וְאֹתוֹ יָלְדָה אַחֲרֵי אַבְשָׁלוֹם *And him she*
had borne (Should we not read יָלַד *he had begotten*?)
after Absalom (1 Kings i. 6).

III. Wāw Consecutive is naturally not used when it
is necessary to emphasize the simultaneity of two actions
or states, in which case two parallel clauses in which the
Nominative stands first[1] are coupled together by simple

---

[1] Occasionally however when the clause contains a word, other than
the verb. which must stand first, the Nominative is omitted: e.g.

wāw. This construction is found not only with the Perfect but also with the Imperfect and the Participle, and even when one clause does not contain a verb: e.g.

הַשֶּׁמֶשׁ יָצָא עַל־הָאָרֶץ וְלוֹט בָּא צֹעֲרָה

As the sun rose upon the earth, Lot came to Zoar
(Gen. xix. 23)

הֵמָּה עֹלִים בְּמַעֲלֵה הָעִיר וְהֵמָּה מָצְאוּ נְעָרוֹת

As they were going up the ascent to the city, they[1] met
some damsels (1 Sam. ix. 11)

הִנֵּה עוֹדָךְ מְדַבֶּרֶת שָׁם עִם־הַמֶּלֶךְ וַאֲנִי אָבוֹא אַחֲרַיִךְ

Lo, while thou art there speaking with the king, I will
come in after thee (1 Kings i. 14)

If it is necessary to connect two such clauses with what precedes, this is done by placing before them וַיְהִי, if the reference is to the past, וְהָיָה, if the reference is to the future: e.g.

וַיְהִי הֵמָּה הֹלְכִים הָלוֹךְ וְדַבֵּר וְהִנֵּה רֶכֶב אֵשׁ

And it came to pass that, as they were going along and
talking, lo, there was a chariot of fire (2 Kings ii. 11)

וְהָיָה אֲנִי אֵלֵךְ מֵאִתָּךְ וְרוּחַ יהוה יִשָּׂאֲךָ

And it will come to pass, I shall no sooner go away from
thee than the Spirit of Jehovah will carry thee off
(1 Kings xviii. 12)

טֶרֶם יִשְׁכָּבוּ וְאַנְשֵׁי הָעִיר......נָסַבּוּ עַל־הַבַּיִת *They had not yet gone to*
bed, and (Anglice *when*) *the men of the city beset the house* (Gen. xix. 4).

[1] The use of הֵמָּה in the second clause is merely for the sake of making this clause begin with the Nominative, as is usual in this idiom. In such a case there is no emphasis on the pronoun.

THE PARTICIPLE.

The Participle like the other verbal forms is altogether
timeless.   It is in fact a noun agent, and indeed the most
usual form in which the noun agent occurs.   Thus we not
only find many common nouns which exist in Hebrew
only in a participial form, e.g. מַזְכִּיר, מוֹשֵׁל, אוֹהֵב, אוֹיֵב,
שׁוֹפֵט, מֵינֶקֶת etc., but in the case of stative verbs the
participle is usually identical with the adjective, e.g.
מָלֵא, זָקֵן etc.

Now although a noun agent is in most languages
generally used to denote some permanent occupation or
characteristic, it is manifest that this is not always the
case.   A man, for example, may be called a regicide,
though the murder of kings does not constitute his chief
occupation.   In such a case the noun agent 'regicide' is
merely used to denote that the man so described is distinguished from other men by the fact that he is in some
way or other connected with the murder of a king, though
the time of the murder is in no wise specified.   But if a
man is described as being, say, a ruler on some definite
occasion, we naturally connect the action of ruling with
that occasion, and indeed, since there is nothing to denote
the completion or development of the action, we understand it as *continuing*.   Thus to say that a certain thing

happened when Quirinius was governor is equivalent to saying that it happened while he was governing ; in other words our attention is directed neither to the completion of the act of government, nor to its development from stage to stage, but to its mere continuance.

This sense, however, of the continuance of an action must be regarded as a development, though a very natural one, from the primary sense of the Participle, which merely denotes the agent, or in the case of a Passive Participle, the sufferer of an action which is in no way defined as to time or state.

The Participle is thus used to denote the agent or sufferer of some verbal action, whether

(*a*)   habitual: e.g.

יְהוָֹה מֵמִית וּמְחַיֶּה

Jehovah killeth and preserveth alive (1 Sam. ii. 6)

יְהוָֹה אֱלֹהֵיכֶם הוּא הַנִּלְחָם לָכֶם

Jehovah your God, He it is that fighteth for you
(Deut. iii. 22)

or

(*b*)   of isolated occurrence, both

(*a*)   with reference to some one special act in the past, present or future, in which case the Participle will naturally be definite: e.g.

אֲנִי יְהוָֹה הַמַּעֲלֶה אֶתְכֶם מֵאֶרֶץ מִצְרָיִם

I am Jehovah who brought you up from the land of Egypt
(Lev. xi. 45)

וִיהוֹשֻׁעַ בִּן־נוּן וְכָלֵב בֶּן־יְפֻנֶּה הָיוּ מִן־הָאֲנָשִׁים הָהֵם
הַהֹלְכִים לָתוּר אֶת־הָאָרֶץ

*Now Joshua the son of Nun and Caleb the son of Jephunneh
were of the number of those men who went to spy out
the land* (Num. xiv. 38)

פִּי הַמְדַבֵּר אֲלֵיכֶם

It is my mouth that speaks to you (Gen. xlv. 12)

אַנְשֵׁי עֲנָתוֹת הַמְבַקְשִׁים אֶת־נַפְשֶׁךָ

The men of Anathoth who seek thy life (Jerem. xi. 21)

הַמֵּתָה תָמוּת וְהַנִּכְחֶדֶת תִּכָּחֵד

*That which shall die may die, and that which shall
perish may perish* (Zech. xi. 9)

הַמְדַבֵּר אֵלַיִךְ וַהֲבֵאתוֹ¹ אֵלָי

The man who shall speak to thee (i.e. if any one speak
to thee), *thou shalt bring him to me*
(2 Sam. xiv. 10)

and

(β) with reference to some action in connexion
with the main narrative, in which case it corresponds to
our Participle: e.g.

הֵמָּה הֹלְכִים הָלוֹךְ וְדַבֵּר

They were going along, talking as they went
(2 Kings ii. 11)

הִנֵּה אָנֹכִי נִצָּב עַל־עֵין הַמָּיִם

Behold, I am standing beside the well (Gen. xxiv. 13)

---

¹ כצ״ל.

N.B. 1. When it is necessary to negative an act in a state of continuance, אַיִן (אֵין), not לֹא, is used with the Participle: e.g. אֵינֶנִּי שֹׁמֵעַ *I am not* (or *shall not be* or *was not*) *hearing;* literally *I am not, shall not be, was not, present as a hearer.*

2. When it is desired to mark to some extent the time of an action, and at the same time to represent it as continuing, the verb הָיָה is sometimes used with the Participle: e.g. וְהַנַּעַר הָיָה מְשָׁרֵת אֶת־יְהוָה *And the boy was ministering to Jehovah* (1 Sam. ii. 11), וִיהִי מַבְדִּיל *that it may be* (continually) *dividing* (Gen. i. 6).

3. When the definite article is used with a predicative Participle, it has the effect of emphasizing the Nominative. Thus, for example, the phrase עֵינֵיכֶם הָרֹאֹת (Deut. iv. 3) literally *Your eyes are those that see, have seen etc.*, means *It is your own eyes that have seen.* This idiom may be explained as follows: הָרֹאֹת implies certain definite eyes that see; these are stated to be עֵינֵיכֶם.

THE INFINITIVE.

There are two forms of the Infinitive in common use in Hebrew, the one, the so-called Infinitive Construct, corresponding roughly to the Infinitive of the Greek; the other, the Infinitive Absolute, altogether idiomatic and peculiar to the Hebrew. Both these forms are nouns of action, undefined as to time, person and state. The difference between them lies in the method of their use and not in their essential meaning.

THE INFINITIVE CONSTRUCT.

The name 'Infinitive Construct' is somewhat misleading. It suggests that the form which is so called is the construct state of the Infinitive Absolute, whereas in the Ḳal always, and to some extent in the other conjugations, the two Infinitives are derived from different stems[1]. Moreover the Infinitive Construct, though frequently used in the construct state, is also very commonly found when no Genitive follows it. But unsuitable as the name is, it is so familiar, that any change would cause confusion.

---

[1] Thus the Infinitive Absolute קָטוֹל arises from *ḳaṭâl*, the Infinitive Construct קְטֹל from *ḳṭul* or *ḳuṭl*.

The Infinitive Construct, being a noun of action, can naturally be followed by a *subjective* Genitive[1], e.g. הֲרִימִי *my lifting up*, עׇזְבֵךְ *thy forsaking*, עֲשׂוֹתוֹ *his making* etc. At the same time it possesses sufficient verbal force to allow it to govern an Accusative: e.g. לַעֲשׂוֹת אֶת־יוֹם הַשַּׁבָּת *to keep the Sabbath day* (Deut. v. 15).

I. The Infinitive Construct being an abstract noun of action may occur as the subject of a sentence: e.g.

$$\text{רַע וָמָר עׇזְבֵךְ אֶת־יהוה}$$

An evil and grievous thing is thy forsaking (Anglice *An evil and grievous thing it is that `thou hast forsaken*) *Jehovah* (Jeremiah ii. 19)

$$\text{שְׁמֹעַ מִזֶּבַח טוֹב}$$

Obedience is better than sacrifice (1 Sam. xv. 22)

$$\text{לֹא־טוֹב הֱיוֹת הָאָדָם לְבַדּוֹ}$$

It is not well that man should be alone (Gen. ii. 18)

N.B. It is however doubtful whether in such cases the Infinitive Construct should be regarded as the Nominative, since in many exactly similar cases the preposition

---

[1] Whether the Infinitive Construct is ever followed by an *objective* Genitive is doubtful. There is a distinct form for the *Accusative* suffix of the first pers. sing., e.g. לַהֲמִיתֵנִי *to kill me*. We find also לַעֲשׂוֹת אֹתוֹ *to do it*. At the same time it must be admitted that אַהֲבָה and יִרְאָה, which are commonly used as Infinitives Construct of the verbs אָהֵב and יָרֵא, and which ordinarily govern the Accusative, may be followed by an objective Genitive: e.g. וְאַהֲבַת חֶסֶד *and to love kindness* (Micah vi. 8), יִרְאַת יהוה *the fear of Jehovah* (Isaiah xxxiii. 6).

לְ occurs with the Infinitive: e.g. טוֹב בְּעֵינֵי יהוה לְבָרֵךְ
אֶת־יִשְׂרָאֵל *It was good in Jehovah's eyes to bless Israel*
(Num. xxiv. 1). The rule indeed seems to be that, if the
Infinitive stand before the טוֹב, it is used without the לְ,
but if it stand after, it may be used with or without the
preposition. See 1 Sam. xv. 22, Prov. xvii. 26, xviii. 5.
Perhaps however in such cases the preposition לְ has
become part and parcel of the Infinitive as *to* in English:
cf. Rom. vii. 18 *To will is present with me.* The Infinitive
Construct seems never to occur as the Nominative to a
finite verb.

II. More commonly however the Infinitive Construct
is used objectively, being governed either by a verb or by
a preposition. In such cases, although there is no change
in the essential meaning of the Infinitive Construct, the
translation of it in English will vary considerably, it being
sometimes necessary to translate it by an abstract verbal
noun, as for example when it is followed by a subjective
Genitive, sometimes by the ordinary Infinitive, as when
it is followed by an Accusative. Thus we find it used

(*a*) as the direct object of a verb: e.g.

יָדַע לֶכְתְּךָ אֶת־הַמִּדְבָּר הַגָּדֹל הַזֶּה

He knows thy traversing (Anglice *how thou didst traverse*)
this great wilderness (Deut. ii. 7)

לֹא־זָכַר עֲשׂוֹת חָסֶד

He thought not of kind dealing (Ps. cix. 16)

חָפַצְתִּי צַדְּקֶךָ

I am pleased to justify thee (Job xxxiii. 32)

וּמַה־יָכֹלְתִּי עֲשׂוֹת כָּכֶם

And what was I able to do in comparison of you?
(Judges viii. 3)

לֹא־אָבוּ שְׁמוֹעַ תּוֹרַת יהוה

They would not hear Jehovah's law (Isaiah xxx. 9)

וַיְבַקֵּשׁ הֲמִיתוֹ

And He tried to kill him (Ex. iv. 24)

הַחִלֹּתִי תֵּת לְפָנֶיךָ

I have begun to set before thee (Deut. ii. 31)

(b) governed by a preposition : e.g.

אַחֲרֵי רְאוֹתִי אֶת־פָּנֶיךָ

After I have seen (literally *after my seeing*) *thy face*
(Gen. xlvi. 30)

יַעַן עֲשׂוֹתְכֶם אֶת־כָּל־הַמַּעֲשִׂים הָאֵלֶּה

Forasmuch as ye do (literally *because of your doing*)
all these deeds (Jerem. vii. 13)

וּלְמַעַן הָקִים אֶת־הַדָּבָר

And in order to perform the word (Deut. ix. 5)

וְעַל נַסֹּתָם אֶת־יהוה

And because of their putting Jehovah to the test
(Ex. xvii. 7)

בִּרְאֹתוֹ אֶת־הַמַּלְאָךְ

When he saw (literally *in his seeing*) *the angel*
(2 Sam. xxiv. 17)

וְכִבַּדְתּוֹ מֵעֲשׂוֹת דְּרָכֶיךָ

*And thou wilt honour Him rather than carry out thy
own doings* (Isaiah lviii. 13)

הוּא הֵחֵל לִהְיוֹת גִּבֹּר בָּאָרֶץ

He began to be a mighty man in the land (Gen. x. 8)

חָפֵץ יהוה לַהֲמִיתָם

Jehovah intended to put them to death (1 Sam. ii. 25)

וְלֹא יָכְלוּ לְשֶׁבֶת יַחְדָּו

And they were not able to dwell together (Gen. xiii. 6)

וַתֵּלֶךְ לָקַחַת

And she went to fetch some (1 Kings xvii. 11)

N.B.   1.   It must be remembered that the preposition
לְ is used in Hebrew in a much wider sense than *to* in
English; for example לֶאֱמֶת means *in truth, truthfully*.
Accordingly the Infinitive Construct with the preposition
לְ is frequently used in cases where it cannot be translated
by the English Infinitive: e.g. לֵאמֹר literally *in saying*.
On the other hand with the exception given above, § 1.
note, in every case where the English Infinitive would
be used the Infinitive Construct with the preposition לְ
may be used in Hebrew.

2. When it is necessary to negative an Infinitive Construct with לְ this is effected by the use of לְבִלְתִּי instead of לְ: e.g. וַיִּבֶן אֶת־הָרָמָה לְבִלְתִּי תֵּת יֹצֵא וָבָא וגו׳ *And he built Ramah so as to allow none to go out or come in* etc. (1 Kings xv. 17), וְהָאִישׁ אֲשֶׁר יַעֲשֶׂה בְזָדוֹן לְבִלְתִּי שְׁמֹעַ אֶל־הַכֹּהֵן *And the man who shall act presumptuously in not hearkening to the priest* (Deut. xvii. 12).

3. When the Infinitive Construct is the direct object of a finite verb, the agent of the action expressed by the Infinitive is usually the same as the subject of the finite verb, and the Infinitive therefore needs no definition as to the agent. But when the Infinitive is subordinated by a preposition, it is frequently necessary to define the agent, and this is done by placing a subjective Genitive immediately after the Infinitive Construct: see above, § II. (*b*), examples from Gen. xlvi. 30, Jerem. vii. 13, etc. That the agent in such cases is the subjective Genitive there can be little doubt, but after the decay of the case-endings in Hebrew the exact nature of the construction became obscured, and the Accusative or some other word is sometimes inserted between the Infinitive Construct and its Genitive: e.g. וַיָּשֶׂם יְהוָה לְקַיִן אוֹת לְבִלְתִּי הַכּוֹת־אֹתוֹ כָּל־מֹצְאוֹ *And Jehovah appointed to Cain a sign, to the intent that any one who might meet him should not slay him* (Gen. iv. 15), לָנֻס שָׁמָּה רוֹצֵחַ *That a homicide might flee thither* (Deut. iv. 42). It is however not impossible that in such cases the noun defining the

Infinitive Construct is added as an afterthought and is
to be regarded as a *casus pendens*.

III. By a slight extension of the foregoing usages
the Infinitive Construct with the preposition לְ is employed to denote actions as being necessary, desirable,
possible, or about to take place, and in late style it is
even combined with the conjunction וְ in lieu of a finite
verb. Examples are

מֶה לַעֲשׂוֹת לָךְ הֲיֵשׁ לְדַבֶּר־לָךְ אֶל־הַמֶּלֶךְ

*What can be done for thee?   Can the king be spoken to
concerning thee*[1]*? (2 Kings iv. 13)*

וַיְהִי הַשֶּׁמֶשׁ לָבוֹא

And it came to pass[2]*, the sun was just setting*
(Gen. xv. 12)

וְכִי־אֲנַחְנוּ מְקַטְּרִים* לִמְלֶכֶת הַשָּׁמַיִם* וּלְהַסֵּךְ לָהּ נְסָכִים

*And when we burn sacrifices to the queen of heaven, and
pour out libations to her etc.* (Jerem. xliv. 19)

N.B. To negative such sentences both לֹא and אֵין
are employed: e.g. לֹא לְהַזְכִּיר בְּשֵׁם יהוה *Jehovah's name*

---

[1] Compare the phrase 'This house *to let*' and the North-country
idiom 'What is *to do* with so-and-so?'

[2] That וַיְהִי is used in its common meaning, and that הַשֶּׁמֶשׁ is not
the Nominative to it, is proved by *v.* 17 where הַשֶּׁמֶשׁ is construed as
feminine.

[3] Point thus.

must not be mentioned (Amos vi. 10), אֵין לָבוֹא אֶל־שַׁעַר הַמֶּלֶךְ *It was impossible to enter the king's gate* (Esther iv. 2).

The use of the Infinitive described in the foregoing section belongs, however, rather to a treatise on Hebrew syntax than to a description of the Hebrew tenses, since in every case the Infinitive Construct retains its essential meaning.

THE INFINITIVE ABSOLUTE.

The Infinitive Absolute is, as stated above, peculiar to the Hebrew. Leaving out of account a few instances in which it takes the place of the Infinitive Construct after another verb, where the Infinitive Construct should probably be restored, its usage is altogether idiomatic.

I. Since the Infinitive Absolute denotes the mere action of the verb without any limitation of time, person, or state, it is frequently used in addition to the finite verb, which it generally precedes but sometimes follows, in order to emphasize the purely verbal notion. In practically every case the meaning conveyed by it can, by an intelligent reader, be represented in English by the mere emphasis; though in order to leave no doubt as to the exact meaning of a translation, it is frequently desirable to render it by some adverb. It may in fact be said that whatever meaning is capable of being conveyed by the emphasis on an English verb may be expressed in Hebrew by the addition of the Infinitive Absolute. Thus it may express solemn assurance or warning, impatience, surprise etc., contrast with another action; or it may imply that the action is in some way limited to the verb which it qualifies. The context will always be a sufficient guide to its exact shade of meaning. Examples are

שׁוֹב אָשׁוּב אֵלֶיךָ

I will return to thee (Gen. xviii. 10).

וְהָמֵת אַל־תְּמִיתֻהוּ

And on no account slay it (1 Kings iii. 26)

הָאֶחָד בָּא־לָגוּר וַיִּשְׁפֹּט שָׁפוֹט

*The fellow came here alone as an uitlander and now he
has turned judge !!* (Gen. xix. 9)

שָׁאוֹל שָׁאַל הָאִישׁ לָנוּ וּלְמוֹלַדְתֵּנוּ......הֲיָדוֹעַ
נֵדַע כִּי יֹאמַר וגו׳

*Well, but the man actually asked about us and our kindred......
Were we to know* (Anglice, *How were we to know*) *that he
would say etc.?* (Gen. xliii. 7)

וְלֹא אָבִיתִי לִשְׁמֹעַ לְבִלְעָם וַיְבָרֶךְ בָּרוֹךְ אֶתְכֶם

But I would not listen to Balaam, and he blessed you
(Joshua xxiv. 10)

[The emphasis on the word *blessed* is to bring out the
contrast with Balaam's intention of cursing.]

טָעֹם טָעַמְתִּי......מְעַט דְּבַשׁ

I only just tasted......a little honey (1 Sam. xiv. 43)

שִׁמְעוּ שָׁמוֹעַ אֵלַי וְאִכְלוּ טוֹב

Only hearken unto me, and ye shall enjoy[1] prosperity
(Isaiah lv. 2)

וְאִם־אָמֹר יֹאמַר הָעֶבֶד וגו׳

But if, on the other hand, the slave shall say etc.
(Exodus xxi. 5)

---

[1] For this use of the Imperative see above, on the Cohortative,
Jussive and Imperative, § IV.

אִם־נָתֹן תִּתֵּן אֶת־הָעָם הַזֶּה בְּיָדִי וְהַחֲרַמְתִּי אֶת־עָרֵיהֶם

If Thou wilt only give this people into my hand, I will
destroy their cities (Num. xxi. 2)

וְאֵת שְׂעִיר הַחַטָּאת דָּרֹשׁ דָּרַשׁ מֹשֶׁה וְהִנֵּה שֹׂרָף

And Moses inquired indeed for the sin-offering goat, and
lo, it had been burnt (Lev. x. 16)

[The Infinitive Absolute in this sentence implies that
Moses could do no more than inquire, since the goat was
not forthcoming.]

הָלוֹךְ הָלְכוּ הָעֵצִים לִמְשֹׁחַ עֲלֵיהֶם מֶלֶךְ

The trees went to anoint over them a king (Judges ix. 8)

[The meaning of the emphasis here seems to be that
the trees started with a certain purpose, but, as the fable
shews, this purpose was unsuccessful.]

N.B.   The explanation of this use of the Infinitive
Absolute seems to be as follows.   Hebrew possesses but
few particles, and makes good its deficiency in this respect
entirely by the emphasis.   Unfortunately this is a matter
to which translators have as yet given practically no
attention.   Not only is the whole force of many passages
entirely overlooked through this neglect of the emphasis,
but translations are frequently suggested, especially in the
book of Job, which absolutely ignore the emphatic word,
and depend for their meaning on the supposed emphasis
on some word that in the Hebrew is altogether without
emphasis.   Under ordinary circumstances the first word
in a sentence is most emphatic, and as in a normal
sentence the chief emphasis falls on the verb, it naturally

occupies the first place. It frequently happens however that it is necessary to put some extra emphasis on the verb, and since it is manifest that this cannot be done by altering its position, it can only take place by the addition of some word. Now a finite verb consists of two parts, either of which may require to be emphasized. If it is desired to emphasize the person, this is naturally done by the addition of a personal pronoun. If, on the other hand, it is necessary to lay stress on the action, the Infinitive Absolute, which expresses the mere action of the verb undefined as to time, person or state, is employed in addition to the finite verb, and qualifies it as an adverbial Accusative. In such cases the Infinitive Absolute is usually, but not necessarily, of the same conjugation as the finite verb.

II. By a slight extension of the foregoing usage two Infinitives Absolute are commonly coupled together to express simultaneous actions qualifying that of a finite verb or participle. In this case one of the Infinitives will be from the same root as the finite verb. Examples are

וַיֵּלֶךְ אִתָּהּ אִישָׁהּ הָלוֹךְ וּבָכֹה

And her husband went with her, weeping as he went
(2 Sam. iii. 16)

שָׁלַחְתִּי אֲלֵיהֶם אֶת־עֲבָדַי הַנְּבִיאִים הַשְׁכֵּם וְשָׁלֹחַ

I sent unto them my servants the prophets from the beginning onward (literally *starting early and sending*)
(Jerem. xxix. 19)

הָלוֹךְ וְטָפֹף תֵּלַכְנָה

Mincing along they go (Isaiah iii. 16)

III. By a similar usage the Infinitive Absolute is frequently employed adverbially to qualify the action of a preceding verb, though the Infinitive Absolute of that verb is not expressed. This is especially common in the case of הֵיטֵב, מַהֵר and הַרְבֵּה which have in fact become mere adverbs. The following are examples:

$$\text{וָאֶכֹּת אֹתוֹ טָחוֹן הֵיטֵב}$$

And I beat it to atoms, grinding it thoroughly
(Deut. ix. 21)

$$\text{סָרוּ מַהֵר מִן־הַדֶּרֶךְ}$$

They have quickly turned aside from the way (Ex. xxxii. 8)

$$\text{יֵהוּא יַעַבְדֶנּוּ הַרְבֵּה}$$

Jehu shall serve him much (2 Kings x. 18)

IV. The Infinitive Absolute is used interjectionally to express the wish of the speaker, generally as an Imperative, but occasionally perhaps as a Cohortative or Jussive[1]. This usage, however, which is especially common with the verb הלך, occurs more frequently in the silver

---

[1] This last usage is a little doubtful from the paucity of illustrations. There are indeed only three passages in which it seems necessary to understand an Infinitive Absolute as equivalent to a Cohortative or Jussive, viz. 1 Kings xxii. 30 (quoted p. 91), Num. xv. 35, Prov. xvii. 12. Another difficulty presents itself in the last two of these passages in the fact that the Infinitive Absolute is coupled with a Nominative. In Num. xv. 35 כָּל־הָעֵדָה may be explained as due to an afterthought, added in order to take away any ambiguity. This explanation will not however serve in the case of the passage from Prov. xvii. 12, and it is possible that here and in 1 Kings xxii. 30 the text needs correction.

age of Hebrew, i.e. the period subsequent to Isaiah and
Micah. Examples are

לָקֹחַ אֵת סֵפֶר הַתּוֹרָה הַזֶּה

Take this law-book (Deut. xxxi. 26)

הָלוֹךְ וְרָחַצְתָּ

Go and wash (2 Kings v. 10)

אָכוֹל וְשָׁתוֹ כִּי מָחָר נָמוּת

Eat and drink, for to-morrow we shall die (Isaiah xxii. 13)

הִתְחַפֵּשׂ וָבֹא בַמִּלְחָמָה

I will disguise myself and go into the battle
(1 Kings xxii. 30)

V. The Infinitive Absolute is used to denote actions
of which it is unnecessary to specify the agents or state;
either because these have been already sufficiently indi-
cated or because the actions are purely general: e.g.

אָלֹה וְכַחֵשׁ וְרָצֹחַ וְגָנֹב וְנָאֹף פָּרָצוּ וגו'

They commit perjury (literally *swear and lie*) *and murder
and steal and commit adultery, they break out etc.*
(Hosea iv. 2)

[In this sentence the Infinitives are in reality a series
of nouns, as much as to say 'There is perjury etc.']

כֹּה אָמַר יהוה אָכוֹל וְהוֹתֵר

Thus saith Jehovah, They shall leave after eating
(2 Kings iv. 43)

הֲגָנֹב רָצֹחַ וְנָאֹף וְהִשָּׁבֵעַ לַשֶּׁקֶר וְקַטֵּר לַבַּעַל וְהָלֹךְ

אַחֲרֵי אֱלֹהִים אֲחֵרִים......וּבָאתֶם וַעֲמַדְתֶּם לְפָנַי

Are you to steal, murder, and commit adultery and perjure
yourselves, and burn sacrifice to Baal, and follow other
gods......and then come and stand before Me?

(Jerem. vii. 9, 10)

וְעַתָּה אוֹדִיעָה־נָּא אֶתְכֶם אֵת אֲשֶׁר־אֲנִי עֹשֶׂה לְכַרְמִי

הָסֵר מְשׂוּכָּתוֹ וְהָיָה לְבָעֵר פָּרֹץ גְּדֵרוֹ וְהָיָה לְמִרְמָס

And now I will tell you what I am going to do to my
vineyard : I shall take away its hedge, so that it shall
be browsed upon ; I shall pull down its wall, so that it
shall be trampled down (Isaiah v. 5)

וְזֶה־לְּךָ הָאוֹת אָכוֹל הַשָּׁנָה סָפִיחַ

And this will be the sign for thee ; ye shall eat (i.e. there
shall be an eating) *this year that which is self-sown*

(2 Kings xix. 29, Isaiah xxxvii. 30)

בְּזֹאת יִתְהַלֵּל הַמִּתְהַלֵּל הַשְׂכֵּל וְיָדֹעַ אוֹתִי

Whosoever will boast, let him boast in this, that he under-
stands and knows Me (Jerem. ix. 23)

VI. The Infinitive Absolute is likewise used in
narration in lieu of the Perfect or Imperfect with Wāw
Consecutive, when the time and the person have been
made sufficiently clear by a preceding finite verb. This
usage however can hardly be considered an elegance, and
belongs to the later period. Examples are

וַיַּפְקִדוּ אֶת־יִרְמְיָהוּ בַּחֲצַר הַמַּטָּרָה וְנָתֹן לוֹ
כִּכַּר־לֶחֶם לַיּוֹם

And they committed Jeremiah to the Court of the Guard,
and gave him a loaf of bread a day
(Jerem. xxxvii. 21)

זְרַעְתֶּם הַרְבֵּה וְהָבֵא מְעָט אָכוֹל וְאֵין־לְשָׂבְעָה שָׁתוֹ
וְאֵין־לְשָׁכְרָה לָבוֹשׁ וְאֵין־לְחֹם לוֹ

You have sown much and brought in little; you eat but
cannot satisfy your hunger; you drink but cannot get
mellow; you wrap yourselves up but cannot grow warm
(Haggai i. 6)

שָׂדוֹת בַּכֶּסֶף יִקְנוּ וְכָתוֹב בַּסֵּפֶר וְחָתוֹם וְהָעֵד עֵדִים

They shall buy fields for money, and write deeds, and
seal them, and take witnesses (Jerem. xxxii. 44)

ADDITIONAL NOTE ON THE INFINITIVE.

Any account of the use of the Infinitive in Hebrew is complicated by the fact that, if we are to trust the Masoretic text, the two forms of the Infinitive can be used indifferently except that the Infinitive Absolute cannot take a suffix. Thus we find the Infinitive Absolute used for the Infinitive Construct in the following instances: (a) when governed by another verb: e.g. חִדְלוּ הָרֵעַ לִמְדוּ הֵיטֵב *Cease to do evil, learn to do well* (Isaiah i. 16, 17);

הַשְׁקֵט לֹא יוּכָל *Keep still it cannot* (Isaiah lvii. 20, Jerem. xlix. 23); וְלֹא אָבוּ בִדְרָכָיו הָלוֹךְ *And they would not walk in His ways* (Isaiah xlii. 24); לְדַעְתּוֹ מָאוֹס בָּרָע וּבָחוֹר בַּטּוֹב *When he comes to the knowledge to refuse what is bad and to choose what is good* (Isaiah vii. 15, cf. v. 16); וְהוֹכֵחַ אֶל־אֵל אֶחְפָּץ *And I would state my case to God* (Job xiii. 3); לֹא יִתְּנֵנִי הָשֵׁב רוּחִי *He will not suffer me to draw breath* (Job ix. 18); לֹא יֶאֱהַב לֵץ הוֹכֵחַ לוֹ *A scoffer loves not that one should reprove him* (Prov. xv. 12): (b) apparently as the subject of a sentence: e.g. הֵיטֵיב אֵין אוֹתָם *Well-doing is not with them* (Jerem. x. 5); אָכֹל דְּבַשׁ הַרְבּוֹת לֹא טוֹב *To eat much honey is not good* (Prov. xxv. 27); הַמְשֵׁל וָפַחַד עִמּוֹ *Sovereignty and terribleness are with Him* (Job xxv. 2): (c) when governed by a preposition: e.g. בְּהַנְחֵל עֶלְיוֹן גּוֹיִם *When the most High apportioned the nations* (Deut. xxxii. 8); כִּי תְכַלֶּה לַעְשֵׂר *When thou shalt finish tithing* (Deut. xxvi. 12); בַּעְשֹׂר הַלְוִיִּם *When the Levites take the tithe* (Nehem. x. 39); בְּהַשְׁקֵט וּבְבִטְחָה תִּהְיֶה גְּבוּרַתְכֶם *In keeping quiet and in confidence shall be your might* (Isaiah xxx. 15); וְכִי־אֲנַחְנוּ מְקַטְּרִים ¹ לִמְלֶכֶת הַשָּׁמַיִם וּלְהַסֵּךְ לָהּ נְסָכִים *And when we burn sacrifices to the queen of heaven, and pour out² libations to her* (Jerem. xliv. 19, cf. v. 25); וַיֵּשֶׁב הָעָם לֶאֱכֹל וְשָׁתוֹ *And the people sat down to eat and drink* (Ex. xxxii. 6); לְהַרְבֵּה *in abundance* (Nehem. v. 18); עַד־כַּלֵּה *till an end is made* (2 Kings xiii. 17, 19, Ezra ix. 4); עַד לְכַלֵּה *till they had made an end* (2 Chron. xxiv. 10, xxxi. 1).

It is however remarkable that in most of the above instances the difference between the two Infinitives is merely one of pointing, and moreover a concordance shews that in similar cases the Infinitive Construct is the normal form. Thus לְמַד and חָדַל are elsewhere always followed by the Infinitive Construct with or without the preposition לְ; יֵכַל is elsewhere always construed with the Infinitive Construct, unless עַשֹּׁהוּ (Ex. xviii. 18) be the Infinitive Absolute with a suffix !, and וְנֶחְבָּה (Jerem. xlix. 10) be a mistaken pointing for וְנֶחְבָּה. יָדַע, אָבָה, נָתַן, אָהַב, חָפֵץ (in the sense *to allow*, governing an Accusative of the person) are all elsewhere followed by

---

¹ Point thus.

² For the construction see above, on the Infinitive Construct, § III.

the Infinitive Construct with or without the preposition
לְ. Again, to consider the instances quoted under (*b*), it
is noteworthy with reference to Proverbs xxv. 27 that in
all other similar cases in which טוֹב is the predicate—
with the doubtful exception of הַכֵּר־פָּנִים (Prov. xxiv. 23,

xxviii. 21), which owing to the shortening of the syllable
through the Maḳḳēf may be either the Absolute or the
Construct—the Infinitive Construct is the normal form;
the rule being apparently that, if the Infinitive stand
before the predicate טוֹב, it is used without the preposition
לְ. Moreover as a parallel to the passages quoted from
Jeremiah x. 5 and Job xxv. 2, we find with the Infinitive
Construct וּבְיָדְךָ לְגַדֵּל וּלְחַזֵּק לַכֹּל *And in Thine hand it*
is to make great and to give strength unto all (1 Chron.
xxix. 12). At the same time it must be admitted that in
הַמְשֵׁל (Job xxv. 2) we seem to have a mere abstract
noun of which the verbal force is almost entirely lost, and
it is not improbable that the Infinitive Absolute Hiph'îl
was actually so used in the later stages of the language;
at least this seems to be the natural conclusion from the
occurrence of such nouns as הֶפְסֵד in Rabbinic Hebrew.

In most of the instances quoted under (*c*) it is probable
that the pointing is wrong. In Ex. xxxii. 6, however, we
may possibly have the work of a 'compassionate editor,'
whereas הַרְבֵּה has so completely become an adjective,
that there is no great difficulty in accepting the reading
לְהַרְבֵּה (Nehem. v. 18), though the text is not improbably
corrupt.

On the other hand we find the Infinitive Construct
used for the Infinitive Absolute in הַרְבּוֹת (Prov. xxv. 27),
וְשָׁתוֹת? (Isaiah xxii. 13), אָלוֹת? (Hosea x. 4), וְהַכּוֹת

(2 Kings iii. 24), הֶעֱבִיר (Josh. vii. 7), הָסִיר ,וְהָרִים,
הַשְׁפִּיל (Ezek. xxi. 31), הָיוֹת (Ps. l. 21), חֲבֹל (Neh.
i. 7), וְהַעֲלוֹת (1 Chron. xxi. 24), וְהוֹדוֹת (2 Chron. vii. 3).
It is however noteworthy that הַרְבּוֹת as an adverbial
Infinitive is unique, whereas הַרְבֵּה occurs upwards of forty
times, though, strangely enough, not in Proverbs. The
curious hybrid וְשָׁתוֹת is probably a scribe's blunder, since
וְשָׁתוֹ occurs in the same verse. It is, however, significant
that the Masoretes, notwithstanding the fact that the word
looked like a Construct, pointed it as Absolute. The same
remark applies to אָלוֹת, unless we are to understand it
as the Construct Plural of the noun אָלָה. Hosea elsewhere (chap. iv. 2) uses אָלֹה as the Infinitive Absolute.
In 2 Kings iii. 24 the text is certainly corrupt: the LXX.
read two Infinitives, but whether their MS. had הַכּוּ or
הַכּוֹת it is impossible to say. Perhaps the final ת is due
to the following אֶת. In Ezek. xxi. 31 the pointing is
chaotic: it is scarcely likely that the forms הַנְגְּבֵּה and
הַשְׁפִּיל would be used by the same writer. In Ps. l. 21
the text is uncertain, the LXX. having read הַוּוֹת (cf. Ps.
lvii. 2). חֲבֹל (Neh. i. 7) was probably intended by the
punctuators to be understood as a noun with the same
sense as in Ezek. xviii. 16: in any case the vowels only
are in question. In the two instances from Chronicles a
ל has probably dropped out, and should be restored
according to the idiom described above: see on Infin.
Constr., section III.

It is true that an objection may be made to altering
the Masoretic pointing on the ground that there exist
forms, pointed by the Masoretes as Constructs in accord-
ance with the norm, which would more naturally be

pointed as Absolutes: e.g. נָתֹן־ (Gen. xxxviii. 9), נְתֹן
(Num. xx. 21) as the Infinitive Construct of נתן; הֲלֹךְ
seven times as the Infinitive Construct of הלך; עָשֹׂה,
עָשֹׂו four times for עֲשׂוֹת. But the pointing of these
forms as the Infinitive Absolute would involve the conclusion that the Infinitive Absolute can be used with the
prepositions לְמַעַן, מִן, לְ, לְבִלְתִּי; and in the face of the
great number of cases in which these prepositions govern
forms which can only be the Construct, it would be
difficult to accept such a supposition.   Great as the work
of the Masoretes undoubtedly is, it is impossible to shut
our eyes to their numerous vagaries.   The men who
pointed, for example, יְרָאתֶם (Joshua iv. 24), even though
in this instance we can find a motive for the pointing in
Jewish exclusiveness, were, from a grammatical point of
view, capable of anything!

INDEX OF PASSAGES QUOTED OR REFERRED TO.

For EU product safety concerns, contact us at Calle de José Abascal, 56–1°,
28003 Madrid, Spain or eugpsr@cambridge.org.

www.ingramcontent.com/pod-product-compliance
Ingram Content Group UK Ltd.
Pitfield, Milton Keynes, MK11 3LW, UK
UKHW020312140625

459647UK00018B/1842